D1315472

Honoré de Balzac

Introduced by
Françoise d'Eaubonne

34.

Minerva

97
B2
Ba12

843.701
D34h

An album by
Pierre Waleffe

Translated by
Adel Negro

HIGHLAND COMMUNITY
JUNIOR COLLEGE LIBRARY
HIGHLAND, KA SAS

72.3-351

© Editions Minerva Genève, 1969

© *Editions Hermès, Paris, 1966*

PHD

On May 21, 1799, in the year of the eighteenth of Brumaire, the registrar drew up the birth certificate of Honoré Balzac, son born to Bernard-François Balzac and his lawful wife, Anne Charlotte Laure, née Sallambier.

True child of his star, the Bull, the little Honoré exhibited the same prodigious energy, tenacity, ponderousness, and sensuality. In his case, however – and therein lies the transcendence of genius – love of earthly goods so sublimated itself that he preferred the shadow to the glory, and the symbol to the riches themselves.

The Bull, however, is also the sacred animal of Mithra, god of «mana» and of the waters of life which assumed so great an importance in Balzac's thought. On his hairy, brutal forehead, the cosmic Bull bears the solar disk, the huge wheel of flame that moves the worlds. Balzac carried this intensity in his eyes, those fiery spheres declared admirable even by his enemies.

Originally, Balzac's father was named «Balssa.» Son of southern vine cultivators, he arrived in Paris with a smattering of Latin and left obscurity to meet his fortune in the Revolution. Enriched by the war (he was made military intendant at Tours), he proposed in 1809 to erect to Napoleon's honor «a statue as big as the Colossus of Rhodes»!

Balzac's mother, who had had some instruction, was the daughter of lacemakers whom Honoré would later recall in *La Maison du Chat-qui-pelote*. Of a dry disposition, she shed neither love nor tears on her marriage with the wealthy quinquagenarian who had so impressed these small shop-keepers. Later, she and her mother treated him disdainfully but he paid them no heed. «Gascon hound!», shouted his mother-in-law. «He's a stone around my neck», screamed his wife, forever ready to believe herself the victim of outrage. She bore four children, three of them – Honoré, Laure and Laurence – undoubtedly the offspring of the «Gascon hound». More suspect

3

is the origin of their brother Henri, for whom Mme Balzac exhibited a much greater fondness. Today he is ascribed to the doings of a late suitor, Monsieur de Margonne. Later on, Balzac said of his mother — with some exaggeration in other respects: «She despised me even before I was born.»

Despite the vast patriarchal home and comfortable income, the young Honoré was placed in a nursery until the age of seven, then sent to a somber, dreary boys' school in Vendôme from which he returned in sorry condition. This experience among the Oratorian Brothers later furnished the childhood setting for his hero, *Louis Lambert*. From June 22, 1807 until April 22, 1813, Honoré was walled in that environment. To escape the filth and oppressiveness of three hundred fellow-students, and to forget the smart of a ruler descending on the knuckles, the future novelist fed on literature, devouring books with extraordinary voracity. «As I read about the battle of Austerlitz, I saw all that happened. The cannon volleys and the cries of the soldiers resounded in my ears, stirring me to my very entrails. I smelled the powder, I heard the noise of horses and the voices of men, and I looked in wonder upon the plain where nations in arms clashed together...» Already a visionary, like Louis Lambert in whom he drew his portrait, the little pupil forgot the misery of his condition in the joyous transports of reading.

When his nervous breakdown finally obliged his parents to bring him home, the chubby-cheeked, merry-eyed little boy had become a thin, bewildered, stuttering adolescent of fourteen. He re-encountered his family: like Jupiter reigning with superb indifference, his father ruled over his family and his military supplies trade, at the same time writing his memoirs which, among other moralistic intentions, aimed at the misconduct of maids. (With the help of the cook's daughter, he had given his children a clandestine sister, who died in a hospital many years later.) His mother continued as ever to scold and make scenes, supported by the invincible Grandmother Sallambier. Happily, his sister Laure was there; with her he would climb up to the attic, called «the hold-all,» where he would entrust to her his long secrets. From this storage room the two children watched the Loire flowing along its lovely banks, among the patch-work of roofs glistening beneath the gentle sun of Touraine.

When the child had fully recovered, the Balzacs settled in Paris. Here, Honoré registered at the Faculté of Law after taking private lessons from a friend of his father, a certain Lepître who had been implicated earlier in an adventurous escape attempt by Marie-Antoinette. It was now 1816.

If Honoré at last thought he would have a taste of freedom, he was mistaken. His father, whose business was suffering, forced the boy to support his studies by earning some money as notary clerk to the lawyer Guillonnet de Merville. Fortunately this gentleman was an extremely good-natured sort, indulging the petulance and fancies of his young employee and closing his eyes to the latter's all too frequent absences. In the practice, Honoré rubbed elbows with other future writers: the dramatist Scribe, and Jules Janin who went from errand-boy to celebrated critic. His colleagues named Honoré, «the Elephant.» One day he received a note from his kindly master, begging him not to come, «for there was pressing work»! In fact, Merville later told him laughingly that his chit-chats with Scribe inflicted so great a loss of time on the practice that his presence «amounted to the absence of three clerks»!

Balzac marvelled at everything: the quays, the complicated network of avenues, the stalls of the second-hand booksellers. Eagerly he went to visit the delightful spinster, Mademoiselle Rougemont, a survivor of the Ancien Régime who knew the words of Beaumarchais by heart. In enthusiasm for her, he became a royalist, a sentimental allegiance later to be confirmed by the good Laure de Berny. At the Sorbonne, other rapturous encounters: the philosophy of Villemain and the theories of Victor Cousin.

From 1819 to 1820, a turbulent current of ideas set Paris astir. At this time, Vigny, like Balzac, was twenty years old; Delacroix, Michelet and Auguste Comte, twenty-one; Hugo and Lacordaire, seventeen; Sainte-Beuve and George Sand, fifteen. With no thought of publishing yet, but incapable of resisting the urge to write, Balzac began to produce vague, ardent essays on the immortality of the soul, and commentaries on Malebranche and Descartes. His father wanted him to be a notary. The lawyer Passez, a devoted friend of the father, was getting old; eventually he would leave his career to the young man and the family could retire to the country.

Honoré refused. He would not be a notary, he declared; and to the general horror of his family, he announced for the first time:

— I shall be a writer!

Dismayed and furious, his parents finally consented to a trial; giving him a very small income, they installed him in a garret with the following ultimatum:

— In two years you will give some good proof; if not, you will get no more help from us. Let that be a warning!

To understand such harshness, one must remember that at this time only the man of means, the land-owner or the capitalist, could afford to exercise the writer's profession. Chateaubriand owned a magnificent château in Brittany; Sand lorded over Nohant; Hugo was son of a general of the Empire. But

5

what petty bourgeois would be so bold as to utter the statement made by Honoré?

In the rue Lesdiguière, a step away from the Faubourg Saint-Antoine, Honoré lived under the rooftops like a student out of Mürger. Familiar to him were the colorful images provided by his neighbors, a hardware merchant and several milliners; often he would catch sight of «waves of brown and red tile,» with «moss on the edges,» or «the pretty white arm of a seamstress watering a pot of flowers,» and «the beaked profile of an old woman in her broken casement window.» Shivering with cold in the dead of winter, wielding his feather pen as he sat enveloped in shawls, Honoré knew no relief save that brought occasionally by the little goodies sent to him secretly by his sister Laure. His first literary attempt finally appeared; it was a total failure. He had tried his hand at drama in verse, a genre ill-suited to his talent, and had come up with a ludicrous work, *Cromwell*. When he read it to his family, who for practical reasons now lived in Villeparisis, they raised a storm of protests, declaring him completely mad for having strayed so far from the right course. Without a doubt he should abandon literature. He now returned to live beneath his parents' roof, in the room left by his beloved sister Laure, who had gotten married. He did not renounce his «pipedreams» however; he was as stubborn and ambitious as his father, the obscure peasant who owed his wealth to historical circumstance.

For three years, he blackened page after page with his stories — *Jeanne la Pâle*, *L'Héritière de Birague*, and other extravagant tales of misguided orphans, embezzled inheritances, gloomy adulteries, and mysterious castles. He wrote quickly, much too quickly and carelessly, seeking only to justify his life by earning money as rapidly as possible and reimbursing his family. Walter Scott was in vogue, so he wrote a la Walter Scott.

From the depths of this moral and literary misery, his eyes turned, as if in search of a haven, toward the villa of his lovely neighbors, the women of the Berny family who had also settled in Villeparisis. Their large, well-built house was surrounded by a garden of elms extending to a gently sloping meadow. From this sanctuary emanated the continuous laughter and chatter of very pretty, eligible young women, one of whom the child of adulterous relations between her mother, Laure, and a swarthy Corsican. Honoré composed verses for this «rose of Bengal,» on an old stone bench in a shady cluster of trees. Mme Balzac smiled with satisfaction; her block-head was not so stupid as all that, and the youngest Berny girl was an excellent match, being the daughter of a rich man (but almost blind, as he was subsequently proved). Everyone was wrong, however. No one could possibly suspect that Honoré was drawn to this house several times a day, not by the charming young ladies, but by their mother, already a grandmother and twenty-two years older than Honoré! It was indeed to her that he wrote: «The first time I saw you, my senses were aroused and my imagination so ablaze that I believed you a divinity, though I do not know which one.»

Balzac's work is haunted by this theme of the mature woman who is still desirable, a theme that has won so much success with his readers. The psychological origins of this trait can be traced to the frustation experienced in his childhood with a cold, shrewish mother to whom he forgave nothing. It is what the psychoanalysts call «the weaning complex.» If his mother had been normal and loving, it is more than probable that he would have sought girls of his own age.

After a long resistance, Laure finally succumbed, stupefied by her extraordinary passion. Secretly they met at night; Laure would first open the gates leading to the luxuriant park resplendent in the moonlight, then the doors of her room laden with the fragance of June.

Laure was the daughter of an established family of musicians in Weitzlar, under the patronage of Marie-Antoinette. Her mother, the queen's godchild, was re-married to the bold cavalier of Jarjailles who, with Honoré's former teacher Monsieur Lepître, had planned the evasion of the captive in the Temple. From this touching adventure the good Laure kept a blood-soaked handkerchief and several jewels, precious relics of the queen-martyr. Honoré's imagination was kindled by such memories, and when she described them with emotion, «her face, like a fine cloth the color of camelias, would redden with lovely tones of rose» (Balzac).

Of course, their liaison did not long remain a secret. Furiously, the daughters besieged their mother. To draw him away from «that creature,» Honoré's mother bore down on him with despatch, lecturing vigorously. All in vain; Honoré continued to return. Soon, he included Laure in his work and the writing improved. Thanks to her help, he rapidly became a novelist and for this he was grateful to her until his death.

The increasingly tense situation demanded further sacrifices. Honoré again left his family, going to live in the rue de Tournon near the Luxembourg Gardens, an area full of historic and literary significance. There Laure would go to visit him and to arrange his room. Having made some acquaintance with the world of magazines and reviews, Balzac was bent on being a publisher; it was his latest «whim.» He must at all costs be successful; he must rid himself of his odious family dependence.

His unfortunate experience is well-known; he recounts it in *Les Illusions perdues*. With the courage of a hunted animal, he added a printing shop when the business went into deficit. In eighteen months the nine thousand gold francs (about two thousand dollars) lent to him by Mme de Berny, had been completely dissipated. On the edge of an abyss, he was forced to sell the business to a distant cousin, who took over its liquidation. The printing shop passed into the hands of the Bernys and prospered under the management of the son Alexandre, to whom Balzac had given French lessons as an alibi for his love affair with «Dilecta.» The poor «Dilecta» nevertheless lost forty-five thousand francs in all to the business, and Balzac's parents, forty thousand.

Instead of being utterly crushed by such a defeat, following upon the failure of *Cromwell*, Balzac did not let himself be discouraged. He rented an entire floor, rue Cassini, decorating its walls in attractive, sparkling blue cloth, immediately contracted more debts, and finally set about writing his first work worthy of merit: *Les Chouans*. Undeterred by bankruptcy, he had chosen the furnishings of a lord – richly bound books, soft rugs, marble time-piece with gold inlay. Then, in a new suit of fine cloth ordered from Louviers (which he could no more pay for than the rest), he went off to gather information about «la chouannerie» (insurgent royalism during the Revolution) from his friends, the general Pommereul and his wife, who lived at Fougères.

Jolted about in the general's wicker-cab as they drove through the cobble-stone streets, Balzac brought his inquiries to the survivors of those heroic times when the peasants, ever faithful to the royal lily, combatted the troops of the Republic. He entered their thatch-roofed homes, downed a glass with them, and listened to the vivid tales of old soldiers and wives. These were altogether new and modern methods, never before used by a novelist in France; that year, Balzac became indeed a «reporter.»

The year that saw the appearance of his novel was rich in masterpieces. At the same time, Victor Hugo published *Les Orientales*, Mérimée his *Nouvelles* and *La Chronique de Charles IX*. But Balzac held his own in this company; even his mother was won by a reading of the work.

Following this, he obtained a small, successful flurry of scandal with *La Physiologie du Mariage*, a work which, at that time, appeared madly audacious. It was afterwards that he met the Duchess d'Abrantès, whom he stopped to see in Tours as he returned from Saché, where he had gone to visit Monsieur de Margonne, his mother's former lover. The widow Junot was fifteen years older than the novelist. Small and plump, her skin no longer

Before her death, Mme de Berny ordered that the letters received from Balzac be burned. Above, a scrawled passage in a letter of 1822: «... To love is to feel different from all other men, to feel violently; it is to live in an ideal world, magnificent and splendid among all splendors; it is to know neither time nor divisions, day nor night, winter nor spring.»

young, she still had lovely teeth, beautiful hands, and a look full of fire. Of her former wealth she had kept a stately home in the rue de Montreuil. Lambinet, a journalist with spiteful tongue, described her in her dirty, battered bonnet à la Charlotte Corday, its strings spotted or half-burned by opium cigarettes. Yet, in her ragged old shawl, she could assume all the grace she bore in times past, when she would wear a cashmir cloak of so great a value that her father-in-law, General Junot's father, would advise her to fasten it with a pin, for fear of thieves at the Carrousel fair.

The only great merit of any singular person, in Balzac's opinion, was to have known Napoleon and to be able to speak of him. Since the Duchess was in desperate need of money, Balzac persuaded her to write her Memoirs. So involved were they, and so meandering, that it was said: «Thery are the Memoirs of Mme d'Abracadabrantès.» Balzac's influence is evident. What a spectacle it must have been, those work sessions of two madmen!

Quickly, the passionate stir of memories brought with them a sentimental turn. Mme de Berny became frantic; she had feared younger rivals, or possible marriage. Never had she imagined, however, that she could be beaten on her own territory by a woman only slightly younger than she, or that the great shadow of the Emperor could wrong the memory of Marie-Antoinette! Distraught, she berated her lover for «preventing her from pursuing the uncertain.» Moved, Balzac ceded. At this point, the Duchess fumed and covered the writer with her barbs. He held fast, however, and did not see her again until 1859, when the decline of «Dilecta» had begun.

At this time, he lived in the house, rue Cassini, whose wall of inclosure bore the following legend: *Labsolu, brick merchant*. Fascinated as he was by the symbol of destiny contained in a word, and by bizarre puns, did he, in the face of these words, think of his future hero, Balthasar Claës, in *La Recherche de l'Absolu?*

In the meanwhile, launched by his scandalous book and his love affair with a great lady of the vanished Empire, Balzac was invited into all the salons: he was received by Mme de Récamier between her harp and the large portrait of Mme de Staël, by Delphine Gay, one of the «two most beautiful blondes in Paris» (the other being Mme d'Agoult), and by Marcelline Desborde-Valmore, ugly and shy, but discreet and full of genius. At the home of the Baron Gérard, he encoutered Champollion, Mérimée, Delacroix. From notoriety he went to esteem. But the luxury and sophystication of these salons, «where an insolent pomp parades itself», did not make him forget his pure, strong friendship with an intelligent, virtuous married woman who was to become his mentor. Zulma Carraud, friend of Balzac's sister – now Laure

Surville – lived buried in Issoudun, despite her lively mind and attributes, which would have been ignored by the world had she not met the author of *La Comédie humaine*.

For how much advise and warning would Balzac be indebted to her! For how many moments of encouragement and healthy severity in exchange for despair and gloom! In the company of this small, lame, pretty wife of an obscure captain, he found shelter after each tempestuous affair that ravaged his life – be it woman or creditor. He held an affection for her that neither Mme de Berny nor Mme Hanska ever overshadowed.

A democrat like George Sand, Zulma Carraud brought her desirable influence to bear against more than one woman of rank. Precise and analytic, much more so than the imaginative, fiery, emotional Balzac, she counteracted the harmful effect of those catholic-royalist reveries with which the kind-hearted «Dilecta» had stuffed his golden brain. Humbly Balzac thanked her for helping him «to pull the weeds from his field.» And she answered: «I am the people, the aristocraticized people, but always sympathetic toward those who suffer oppression.»

In the years following the success of *Les Chouans*, Balzac tried his hand at everything, delving into the most diversified of genres and exhausting none. He triumphed again with his *Peau de Chagrin*, one of the most beautiful, romantic utilizations of the dialetic truth: to consume life is to approach death, to see it hastening towards us; and yet, without this consumption, we would not know how to live. This skin of anguish which shrivels with each wish, or rather, with each breath of life, each heart-beat, is this not our own skin?

After 1829, Balzac began his life of «galley-slave of glory,» as he aptly described himself. Dressed in his monk's robe which gave freedom of movement to his powerful bull's neck, he worked only at night, by the strength of the coffee and the light of the candles brought to him by the servant who woke him. On the desk were his crow's feather-pen and his sheets of white paper, tinted lightly with blue. Rolling up his right sleeve like a wood-chopper or a hack driver, Balzac would set to work. Gripped by a living hallucination, he wrote at that well-known, fantastic rhythm, sixteen to seventeen hours without cease, sustained only by his famous coffee every three or four hours. The dose of this marvelous poison, imbibed in torrents while one of the greatest romantic frescos of humanity was being created, has been estimated at fifty thousand cups!

Between his door and that of various printers who transformed his manuscript into a book, there was a constant shuttle of proof-readers, grumblers, and other messengers. They made protests even before the ink had dried on the bundle of paper; they handed him the proof and revisions of a preceding novel, sold even before the first line was written; they harassed him, they groaned about his proliferous corrections, they complained about his delays. Balzac received in his bath like Marat, vociferated like Napoleon, stood his ground, gave orders, stormed, promised, attacked everything and everyone. In a time when the type-writer did not exist, Balzac handed his publishers a mess of scribble. The first proof was returned to him five or six times, sometimes more. Simultaneously, he worked on a new book and signed a contract for a third; each of the works in his *Comédie humaine* had to be re-written, some even seven times.

«Sometimes it seems that my brain is on fire,» he said. «I will die on the pyre of intelligence.» It is not without reason that he has been called the Napoleon of Letters.

In the midst of this infernal existence, he continued to form sentimental relationships, though he did not break with Laure, who remained his prime critic attentive reader and counselor. He now engaged first in a correspondence, then in a flirtation with the unknown beauty who soon revealed herself another of the high-ranking ladies, not of the Empire but of the Ancien Régime: the Marquise de Castries. She was the cream of the bluebloods, daughter of the Duke de Maillé and ex-wife of the grandson of a naval minister. A huge scandal had separated her from Philippe-Hercules de Castries: her adultery with the blond, languishing Victor de Metternich. A noteworthy point: the great Metternich, father of Victor, had been the principal love intrigue of Mme d'Abrantès!

The Marquise had been very beautiful. A contemporary spoke with admiration of her brilliance which «surpassed that of the candles.» She was still slender, with delicate features and a luxuriant mass of blond hair. But she never left her sofa, where she reclined in her cashmir shawl; a fall from the horse, while following her lover on a hunt, had broken her spine. The devout saw in this an act of God.

With the impetuosity of his nature, Balzac fell in love immediately and unreservedly. The clever fellow dreamed only of using this attachment for political ends and so he enlisted his famous pen among those scribbling cohorts whom Zulma Carraud called, with justified scorn, «the domesticity of the Court.» He wrote for the *Rénovateur* in order to break antagonistic lances against the umbrella of the bourgeois-king Louis-Philippe: The sovereign was caught at the time between two hostile extremes: on one side, the Republicans who fired upon him heavily; on the other, the «ultras,» more royalist than the king, who hurled satire and bitter plaints at him. It was thus that Honoré affirmed his ardent aversion to the chimerical equality preached by the horrible current stirred in 1789... the same current which had made his father's fortune and permitted his son to become a writer! He could not renounce his origins, however, and take himself for the queen-martyr's knight-errant; the Marquise rewarded his servility with nothing but small favors instead of the gift of her person, which Honoré had expected as the devotee awaits the grace of God.

In vain he ran after her, like a poodle in the steps of his mistress. He accompanied her to Aix, to Savoy, appearing at her side constantly on excursions. She introduced him to her friends, she even prepared his coffee with her lily-white hands, but of love, nothing. In Geneva, a violent argument broke loose and the poor nonplussed lover fled Switzerland to the arms of his Laure. Her heart, which had already shed so many tears for him, was not closed; on the contrary, it opened even wider, like a mature flower growing fuller after a rainfall.

Honoré now thought only of vengeance, writing his most vindictive novel: *Ne touchez pas à la Hache (Do not handle the hatchet),* later called *La Duchesse de Langeais.* It is the transposition of his aventure with the blond Marquise, the duchess in the story, who finally falls in love with the man she has mocked, then enters a convent and dies there. To savor his revenge more fully, Balzac had the crudeness to read his manuscript to his seductress; the latter, as impassive as Chopin when George Sand made him aware of his ill-treatment under the guise of Prince Karol in *Lucrezia,* manifested a stoic politeness and gave no sign of having recognized herself. And yet, despite his declaration of 1836: «I have broken the last feeble ties of politeness with Mme de Castries,» seven years later, in 1843, he dedicated to her *L'Illustre Gaudissart.*

«When you miss your duchesses, I shall still be there, offering the consolations of true sympathy,» wrote Zulma Carraud after having severely scolded the unhappy dupe.

Even in that moment, fate was about to procure for Balzac a long-lasting revenge which, in the end, was more terrible than defeat, for it resulted in death. The first letter from Mme Hanska had arrived on February 19, 1832, coinciding with the first invitation from Mme de Castries. The letter came from Russia and was signed only with the pseudonym, the Stranger. It was not until long afterwards that Balzac penetrated her black seal, *Diis Ignotis.* As for Laure de Berny, she was now an old woman, driven to desperation by the infidelity of her lover and sorely tried by her family. The illness which would end her days had begun.

Eva Hanska, the enigmatic correspondent, was the wife of the Russian-Polish Baron Waclaw de Hanski, a squire of delicate health who possessed an immense fortune. They lived in Ukraine in complete isolation, far from any asssemblage of society, be it city, town, or even small village; nothing but the miserable huts of serfs lost in oceans of wheat, and beyond these, the forest of birches and oaks. In the midst of this savage nature, their mansion was furnished in a ponderous, sumptuous style: porcelain from China, silverware from Davenport, books from Paris, the paintings of the masters.

The beautiful Eva was bored. She came from an unusual, intelligent family where genius bordered on madness. One of her great-grandfathers had been the illustrious palatine of Kiev, national hero whom the author of *Quo Vadis* placed in one of his novels under the name of Jaréma. One of her brothers was an important political figure; another, a celebrated writer, was called «the Polish Walter Scott.» The natal home resounded with cries and quarrels, whiplashes and slammed doors. The servants were beaten and Eva raised «à la schlague». An ancestor Rzewuska had been decapitated during the Terror; it was said in a half-whisper that on certain nights she descended from her portrait hung in the gallery and walked about, her head under her arm! At nineteen, Eva escaped from this environment by marrying her uncle, the Baron Hanski. Today their revenue would roughly equal one million dollars.

The sole distraction for this Polish lady in Ukraine was the reading of French novels and the begetting of children, all of whom died except one, a girl she loved deeply. One day, with nothing better to do, Eva suggested a good joke to her two nieces and her daughter's governess «Lisotte», a kind, good-natured spinster: Wouldn't it be fun to write to that impertinent Balzac, author of *La Physiologie du Mariage,* just to mystify him? It was necessary for the Countess to involve three other women in the accomplishment of the plan, for her desire, even as a joke, was prohibited by the mores of the time. What would the Count say if he were to find out?

Of course, as soon as the proprieties were safe within this bit of hypocrisy, the correspondence was carried on between Eva Hanska alone and Balzac. The naïve Lisotte, still thinking it an extended joke, served as «mailbox.»

When the masks were finally removed and Balzac learned of the Stranger's great lineage, his imagination immediately caught fire and he fell is love with his «Northern Star» even before seeing her. They must meet one another at all cost. Eva succeeded in convincing her mild husband that he should travel a bit, and so off they set for Neuchâtel where the first encounter had been planned. They would become acquainted, by chance, on the Promenade des Anglais, as agreed. The whole thing must be cloaked in the mystery and precaution of conspirators. If, at present, he knew that he was to meet a wealthy, aristocratic Slav, Balzac did not know either the name or the face of the person for whom he already experienced so violent a passion!

Thus friend Balzac departed in a carriage, abandoning Paris, his debts and his contracts. He traveled with the assumed name of «Marquis d'Entragues.» For Laure and Zulma, his pretext was a certain indispensable document to be found only in Besançon!

As he had been directed, Balzac went to the Villa André, opposite the Hôtel du Faubourg where the Hanskis were staying. Here from a graceful promontory, the city overlooked the spread of blue water where seagulls circled above flickering reflections of liquid gold. On her balcony, Eva Hanska presented a magnificent spectacle: her long black hair unfastened over her shoulders, her exquisite red dress and a single pendant about her neck, a tiny golden tassel with a turquoise, accentuating her striking complexion. Her form was full, her skin fresh, her forehead splendidly chiselled, her mouth perhaps a bit too tight; thus she appeared to the thirty-two year old Balzac in all the brilliance of her thirty-three years.

The encounter occurred with utmost smoothness. The husband suspected nothing; in fact, he was quite flattered by the company of an author whom all of Europe was reading. With George Sand and Victor Hugo, Balzac was the most reputed Parisian author abroad. The couple and their new friend went picnicking on a small island in Lake Bienna; there, in the shade of a large oak, the Polish woman and the Frenchman exchanged their first furtive kisses, while the husband arranged the napkins on the plates. The Napoleon of Letters had found his Maria Walewska.

They promised to see each other again in Geneva, on November 5. Overwhelmed by money and boredom, the elegant lady was unaware of the gaping holes made by these trips in the budget of the «galley-slave of glory,» tormented by his creditors and debts. Then another publisher presented herself, the widow Béchet who saved him for a while.

On November 20, 1833, Balzac had to excuse himself for not flying to Eva's side; he must finish *La Duchesse de Langeais,* write one hundred pages of *Eugénie Grandet* and begin *La Fille aux Yeux d'Or,* a significant work for more than one reason, being the first time in French literature that a case of feminine homosexuality was overtly treated. For this titanic endeavor, Balzac required ten days. And then he wondered that his chair gave way beneath him like a horse under the weight of a warrior!

The projects of the couple became more precise. The divine, the celestial Countess had millions to her name; the husband was an ailing old man with nothing to do but await his death. To Honoré belonged the beautiful widow as well as the Countess. With the poor Hanski still alive, Eva and Honoré united each other in a promise of «betrothal.»

During those days of secret victory, the writer's friends were utterly astounded by his prolific production and ferocious energy. His work capacity defied all limits of the human will. In one hundred nights he had written *La Recherche de l'Absolu*, at the same time commencing his work *Seraphita*, drawn from Swedenborg; in forty days he had created the most popular of his master-pieces, *Le Père Goriot*; in December and in the months following, *La Fille aux Yeux d'Or*. In addition, he had outlined the general scheme of *César Birotteau* and *Le Lys dans la Vallée*. «You are killing yourself,» cried his friend, the Doctor Nacquart.

The entire set of silverware of the rue Cassini was sold so that Balzac could go discuss love with Mme Hanska, in Vienna this time. Here he stayed at the hotel *La Poire d'Or*, where a Pole in one of his novels had just committed suicide! To his immense pleasure, Balzac discovered that the German nobility, unlike that of his own country, was quite understanding, praising him to the skies and hastening to welcome him with every honor. As he suffered the disdain of Mme de Castries, he was unaware that Goethe discoursed with Eckermann about him. The former lover of the Duchess d'Abrantès and father of the Victor who shattered the Castries' hearth, Metternich received Honoré with open arms. The Esterhazys and the Schwarz-enbergs held celebrations in his honor. But alas, upon his return to Paris he found himself on the edge of financial catastrophe; the year 1836 announced itself in the most somber of colors. Even his family became additional anxiety; his sister Laure was sick and depressed; his brother Henri, the natural-born son of Monsieur de Margonne, had returned from India with a wife fifteen years his senior. The taste for older women ran decidedly in the family. As for Mme Balzac, she foundered in a nervous depression that menaced her for the rest of her life. The unfortunate Mme de Berny had steadily worsened; one of her daughters had died, the other was mad. Her days were numbered, ironically at the very moment when her lover magnified her in the book he consecrated to her, *Le Lys dans la Vallée*.

For refusing to stand guard a the Montmartre grape-havest, esteeming that he had better things to do, Balzac was arrested and imprisoned with the workers who had held fast against Louis-Philippe in order not to lose a day or two of salary. Unruffled amid the uproar and calls of the card players, his neighbors in captivity, Balzac continued to write in this «Bean Hotel,» as they had nicknamed the jail. He who had been fêted by all of German nobility and adulated by the intellectual elite of Vienna, who had wooed the multi-millionairess Mme Hanska, manor-lady of Ukraine, now sat calmly revising his proofs among the lowly folk who shared his lot. No man is prophet in his own country!

After this grotesque incarceration his readers, indignant over the fate that befell him, sent to the «*deserter*» Balzac so many jewels that he was able to have one of his seven canes entirely inlaid!

He took up the work-yoke again, without unharnessing; but now another feminine figure appeared on the horizon. In spite of the fidelity he had sworn to Mme Hanska, he could not remain insensible to the charms of so unusual and delightful a woman as the fair-haired Countess Visconti. She had inherited her emerald green eyes and contralto voice from her mother, whose beauty had been renowned and who, in the despair of age, had committed suicide. Two of her brothers had also killed themselves; a sister had succumbed to some mystical madness and another had won notorious reputation for her alcoholism and countless lovers. It was an evil crown that sparkled on Sarah's golden tresses, but she herself was of a sound nature and an easy, frolicsome disposition.

These she manifested not only as lovable mistress, but as the most devoted of friends. While her husband, a gentle maniac, lost himself in music and pharmaceutical research, she dedicated her energies to Balzac's problems, waging battle with him against his creditors and hiding him from them when necessary. One day, when he was hunted out by one of them (like Fra Diavolo caught in the thicket by General Hugo), she forthwith paid his debt of two thousand dollars, thus sparing him another jaunt into prison.

The rue Cassini was now untenable; once again Balzac moved out, going this time to the rue des Batailles (today Avenue d'Iena) under the name of — Mme Durand, widow! At the end of a long dilapidated corridor, beyond two dark, cheerless rooms, he had installed himself in a charming boudoir where sumptuous curtains graced a decor of white, red, and gold, conceived after the interior he described in his sapphic novel, *La Fille aux Yeux d'Or*. Outside, the hens still clucked in the gardens; it was the old village of Chaillot, where one could look out over the lovely slopes of Meudon. Balzac, however, did not waste his time in contemplating the landscape. Like a convict at his labor, he toiled ceaselessly between his candles and his steaming coffee-pot, while the vivid colors of the tapestries and the Turkish divan radiated their brilliance in the light of the silver-gilt chandelier. Here he would receive the visits of a handful of friends, among them Théophile Gautier.

Upon his return from Italy, where he had gone to settle some affairs for the Viscontis in the company of the pretty Caroline Marbouty (a friend of Sainte-Beuve disguised as a boy), Balzac received a cruel blow: the unhappy Laure de Berny had died, alone and overwhelmed by a succession of family misfortunes. How bitterly he repented now of having so neglected her at the very moment when he glowingly painted her portrait in the character of Mme de Mortsauf. He wrote of his grief to Zulma Carraud, to Mme Hanska, to a mysterious Louise of whom we know nothing except that she desired a child by Balzac. «The person I have lost was more than a mother; her only explanation can be found in divinity.» He knew only too well that in the grave of the poor «Dilecta» he also buried his youth. At the same time, summer 1836, he was faced with liquidation and a list of debts amounting to nine thousand dollars.

The creditors bore down on him relentlessly. Evicted from the rue des Batailles as he had been from rue Cassini, Balzac sought refuge in a hotel of the rue de Provence, but even there they hunted him out. Seeing him at his wits' end, the kind-hearted Sarah de Visconti sent him back to Italy for a few days. In 1837, in Turin, wearing a large, soft hat, he posed for a small statue which he later gave to his fair-haired Countess.

The gossips led an active life in this Italian society where the crust of the aristocracy spent its energies on love affairs – in other words, adultery – and on politics – national independence and the struggle against the Austrians. An inquisitive fellow, seeking information on Chateaubriand, reminded Balzac of the biting words uttered by Mme Ancelot:

– He is becoming deaf. That is only natural: he no longer hears what is said of him!

On the way back to France, Balzac was obliged to stop at Genoa. An epidemic was feared and foreigners were being quarantined for forty days. To pass the time, the novelist chatted with a merchant, Giuseppe Pezzi, from whom he learned that a great natural resource was lying neglected in Sardinia: the silver mines. The Romans had exploited no more than a meager portion, so that the greater part of the treasure was still to be conquered. As in the past, Balzac's enthusiasm was kindled; giving the Italian a magnificent description of the enormous exploitation he foresaw, he associated

Imprimerie de H. Balzac,

RUE DES MARAIS S.-G., N° 17.

N° 1 C 3206.

C 3206 Je déclare avoir l'intention d'imprimer un Ouvrage ayant pour titre : La Physiologie du Mariage ou méditations sur le bonheur Conjugal

par M.

faisant un volume in 8° de 20 feuilles environ, tiré à mille exemplaires.

Paris, ce 20 Juillet 1826.

Expédié le 20 Juillet, 1826.

Request for printing authorization: the file in Balzac's printing shop contained 230 such requests, for 24 months and 10 days. This was the first one.

himself with the man and returned to France burning with hopes. In Paris, more military trouble; he was set upon by the National Guard, despite his pseudonym «the widow Brunet.» Once again, they wanted him to stand guard and carry a rifle. That was too much! The exhausted writer moved out, going to «les Jardies» where he had purchased a plot of land and had a small house constructed. He knew and loved Ville-d'Avray where, in former times, he had entertained a certain Olympia, mistress of Rossini. Soon a railroad would pass close-by and the lots would rapidly increase in value; it was certainly an excellent affair.

In his overflowing imagination, the author of *Eugénie Grandet* had already begun to see a tree-shaded little palace, and dreamed of being a speculator, an entrepreneur, a land-owner, and who knows what else. While waiting to begin his exploitations in Sardinia, he planned to grow pineapple, filled the pathways with asphalt, and went into perfect ecstasy about the shrubs no higher than his knee: «Already they prevent me from seeing my dog!» His friends and colleagues who came to visit nearly suffocated in strangled laughter to hear him hold forth on his grandiose projects. Then they would leave, covered with plaster dust, to amuse the high society with the newest stories about «Honoré's latest mania.»

Meanwhile, instead of forwarding the estimates promised after each analysis, Giuseppe Pezzi kept silent. Less loyal and more clever than the Frenchman, the shrewd Italian meant to profit alone from the marvelous project born of a conversation in Genoa.

Suspecting false play, Honoré grew impatient. Leaving his «Jardies» as it was, he made off for Sardinia. Stefan Zweig was justifiably aghast at the improvidence of the expedition, noting that Balzac «brought with him no measuring instrument, no letters of introduction for the authorities; he had called upon no expert's advice, he knew only a few words of Italian, and the basic knowledge of the subject was as lacking as his capital.» (Typical contrast between the scientific, meticulous German mind and the enthusiasm at the base of the southern French character!) But Balzac was so stubbornly determined that he passed five or six sleepless nights in a coach from Paris to Marseille, feeding on milk at six cents a day – a considerable effort for a corpulent man worn out by work and lack of rest. He was forced to make a long detour by way of Corsica, and endured an awful crossing from Toulon to Ajaccio. There he awaited the first boat to carry him to his treasure island. So great was his impatience that he stamped about, and for lack of another pastime, he wielded his cane ferociously at some dogs who had attacked a donkey. Finally, a boat with red sail came into view; it belonged to sponge and coral fishers who took the leaner Balzac on board and nourished him on dried fish throughout the voyage. At last friend Balzac reached Sardinia; and of course he was too late. Pezzi had swindled him; by royal decree he had obtained the right to exploit the «dross.» In order to return to Paris, the illustrious novelist without a cent in his pocket was forced to borrow money in the name of the Viscontis!

The mine affair had been more than sound; it brought enormous wealth to Pezzi and his partners. The unfortunate Balzac, who had conceived the idea (for the information furnished by Pezzi had been nothing more than a banal piece of current conversation) and who received none of its benefits, returned to his beloved «Jardies» to be faced with more debts and a terrible din from all sides. No one had been paid, neither the locksmith nor the upholsterer nor the mason; the soft clay earth gave no support, it couldn't even hold up the gate. Sarah came to live next door so that she could save her lover from disaster. As soon as a bailiff was seen in the distance, the two of them scurried to hide all rugs, chandeliers, bronzes, and porcelains, bringing them all to the home of the Countess. Then, with a tragic gesture, they would indicate to the representative of the law the small desk, the iron bed, and several chairs. No sooner had he gone off than the setting of *La Fille aux Yeux d'Or* reappeared. This continued until the day when one of the miserable wretches discovered the trick that had been played and summoned to court... Sarah's husband!

And that was the end of everything, including his affair with the blond, eccentric Mme de Visconti. The writer sold his property for three thousand dollars; it was to have been his fortune and in fact, it had cost him twenty thousand do dollars! He went to hide in the rue de Passy, on the ground floor where some of his belongings have been gathered to constitute the present-day Balzac museum.

That was 1840; for two more years he trudged on in similar vein, haunted by debts and trying desperately to draw applause with his plays. Each of his books came out of a pit only to open an abyss; surrounded by unpaid luxury which was either confiscated or which he gave to charity, he was poorer now than he had been in his miserable garret, rue Lesdiguière, twenty years earlier. He presented himself before the Academy; he won only the vote of the magnanimous Hugo and that of an obscure member persuaded by Hugo to support Balzac. His desire to be elected deputy was unfulfilled; he wrote plays that were never produced or that were hissed; the newspaper he had launched did not survive. All his life the great writer, celebrated abroad, struggled heavily with failure.

He seriously thought of expatriating himself to Brazil, where reigned a liberal-minded emperor, an admirer of Victor Hugo. And then, from Ukraine came a piece of news bringing with it another drastic influence in his life: Hanski had just died and Eva was now a widow and free!

Huge obstacles, however, rose up between him and the happiness of marrying his «Stranger.» Hanski's will was contested and Eva had to plead at Kiev and at St. Petersburg; then, in order to marry a foreigner, she must apply to the Czar for his authorization.

That was not all, however: there was also a strong family opposition. The proud lineage of the Rzewnskis felt none of the humble admiration for the Letters as evinced by the Germans, nor any of the gracious welcome found in the Italian salons. Instead, the family treated as a *moujik* the writer who falsely called himself «de Balzac.» A certain Aunt Rosalie was the most heated of protestors against Eva's matrimonial projects; she was the daughter of the woman decapitated under the Terror, who supposedly strolled through the corridors of the castle, her bloody head under her arm. To the daughter, the legitimist Balzac, avid supporter of the royal lily, was a Jacobin, a blood drinker, one of those horrible «sans-culotte,» a Frenchman and even worse, a commoner!

Eva hesitated. She thought of her daughter Anna, the only person she had loved sincerely, more than any of her three husbands. What kind of marriage would the girl make if her mother went to live in Europe, as lawful wife of a Frenchman of lowly situation? Furthermore, despite Balzac's genius, the aristocratic Slav had been shocked more than once by his crude cabman's manners, his boisterous voice, his spurious elegance, more like the affected style of a successful valet. There followed a series of dramatic letters; Balzac reproached Eva for her reticence; she hurled at him the infidelities of which all of Europe was aware: the little Marbouty, the fair-haired Sarah. After eighteen months of storm by correspondence, she consented finally to see her *moujik* again.

As they approached each other beneath the elegant ceiling of a Saint Petersburg home, they had not met for *eight years*. A large earthenware stove spread some warmth in the room. Although Mme Hanska had been pregnant seven times, she was still lovely and fresh. Heavier, wearier, Balzac had kept his persuasive eloquence, his violent temperament, his sparkling genius. The two lovers fell into each other's arms with all the passion of former days. Eva asked for a delay: before becoming Mme de Balzac she would like to see Anna well established and settled. Honoré consented and four months later he returned to Paris, happy and pensive.

Nevertheless he began to give signs of pronounced lassitude. Coffee alone no longer sustained him; he drank it «like water.» He wrote *César Birotteau* with his feet soaking in a mustard bath, and *Les Paysans* with his head full of opium. A surprising story!

1844. Hope again rose for the poor, tormented man; Anna Hanska had recently been engaged to an excellent man, Georg Mniszech, and Mme Hanska left her desert to live in Dresden. Would Balzac finally join her? Again an obstacle, this one of a singular kind, making his presence necessary in Paris. He was to make the arrangements for the conversion and entry into the convent of Henriette Borel, «La Lisotte», the Swiss Calvinist who had served as mailbox for Eva and Honoré! At last having realized her role in the affair, she was resolved to expiate her grave sin!

One can easily imagine Honoré's ill-humor at finding himself imposed upon. It was then that Balzac decided to conquer any remaining hesitations of his wild Slavic bird. He would prepare for her the most gilded of cages, and immediately began to save a sum of money to which Eva later added her contribution, in order that they might have a magnificent building in Paris. When at last it was bought, furnished, and decorated, it had cost them sixty thousand dollars. The collection of rare objects planned for his home was Balzac's latest mania, on the same order as those of the silver mines in Sardinia and his property «Les Jardies».

From 1845 to 1847, the perpetual bankrupt sought by every creditor in the city imagined himself a rival of the Louvre, the Hermitage and the palaces. The slightest piece of Dutch porcelaine his eyes fell upon was from China, in his opinion; a small, round landscape, unquestionably a Ruysdael; a twenty-dollar painting, certainly a Holbein! In his morbid need to possess, unaware that he was directing himself toward his ultimate illness, Balzac dreamed of owning an immense wealth all of which he would lay at the feet of «the Stranger.»

He purchased unendingly. He did not stop there but attempted to resell to the king a supposed «dresser of Marie de Médicis», which he then sought to place in the hands of the Baron de Rothschild, and finally the king of Holland, at whose court T. Gautier was to serve as ambassador. It was not the first time that the good Theo became involved in Balzac's chimera; several years earlier Balzac had succeeded in convincing him that thanks to a sleep-walker he had discovered a buried treasure at Pointe-à-Pitre. He wanted to hire a little boat and embark clandestinely with his friend Gautier. After searching their pockets they discovered they barely had enough to buy the shovels needed to unearth the strange treasure!

The cave of Ali Baba, where the author stored all his bric-à-brac, his paintings, canderabra, and furniture bought for Mme Hanska, was the Beaujon home in the rue Fortunée, former mansion of an eighteen-century rake. Pursued by everyone, the poor Honoré longed only for a haven and this he would find solely in union with Mme Hanska. He could no longer finish the works he had begun; for the first time, imagination failed him and he could not get to the end of *Les Paysans,* in spite of siropy coffee, opium and mustard baths.

Brusquely, in 1846, his ardor returned with the inspiration emanating from two recent masterpieces: *Le Cousin Pons* and *La Cousine Bette.* He now no longer bothered about his latest debts, contracted at the tailor's and as a result of a fake bronze acquired at a high sum. Dr. Nacquart was stupified by this old spark of life; in one day alone, on August 12, he had written twenty-four pages. The doctor had ceased long ago to chide this man whom he adored, nor did the extraordinary tailor Brisson insist any more on collecting pay for the frock-coats, suits, dressing jackets and nankeens. Nacquart contented himself with grumbling: «That will inevitably lead to something fatal.» He sensed that the skin of anguish had been stretched to its last limits.

Not so soon! Balzac wished to make the acquaintance of Mme Hanska's intriguing son-in-law. In the spring of 1845, the Northern Juliet called to her side her faded Romeo. While «Lisotte» pursued her strange course, entering the convent of the Visitation (she contributed to Balzac's future image of «Cousine Bette»), the writer enjoyed one of his last periods of leisure in the company of Mme Hanska, her daughter and the charming Georg who removed the last obstacle from Balzac's road to happiness. Balzac adored the lovely young girl, so lively and gracious, with the delicately moulded features of her mother. They all chose colorful names for one another; for the young couple, Balzac became Bilboquet; for Balzac, Georg responded to the nickname Gringalet. A happy, carefree little band, they left for Italy with a sense of abandon, and Eva declared that from then on they should call themselves the *Saltimbanques.* It was a frenetic escapade, a mad European jaunt. Happy at the sight of her happy daughter, Mme Hanska forgot a bit the moralism of a well-brought-up lady and basked in the youthful ardor of the handsome couple.

On his return to Paris, after an audience generously granted to them by the pope, Balzac threw himself headlong into the writing of *La Cousine Bette.* He had taken on a new housekeeper, the worthy Mme de Brugeol; in his passion for nicknames, he called her «the screech-owl,» because of her round eyes and beaked nose. She was to keep constant watch over the small fire burning beneath the coffee-pot of white porcelain marked with purple initials; she was the vestal virgin of the new temple where the flame of literary creation was kindled. Between cups of boiling coffee and fruit, the writer lighted the chiseled bronze of the candlestick until dawn finally extinguished the glow of the tapers. The summer was drawing to its end, parching the lilies of the garden where bees swarmed.

In the course of those pages come General Hulot, greatly aged since *Les Chouans,* the perfect model of senile lust. Poland is represented as a romantic sculptor with flaxen mustache, objet of the secret desires of a spinster, his creditor. The bourgeoisie takes the form of the perfume-dealer Crevel, stupid and vulgar, but of a typically French heroism in the face of death; and for the gallantry of high theft, the perfidious, lovely Mme de Marneffe who dies in atrocious circumstances, killed by the vengeance of a virtuous son Hulot. For his principal character, Bette, Balzac drew his inspiration both from Lisotte and from his poor mother, the old neurotic, Mme Balzac.

From time to time, Balzac would gaze with a sigh at the portrait of Eva, done by Daffinger in Vienna, as if to ask her for inspiration. Then he would take up his pen once more, finish the page and off he'd go to the antique shops where his collector's madness had become a legend.

Unable to stand it any longer, he entrusted his ridiculous treasures to Mme Balzac his mother, entreating her, as the father Grandet to his daughter: «Take good care of everything!» and set off for Ukraine. Anna and «Gringalet» were now legally wed, and nature now came to Balzac's aid with a magnificent argument to hasten the conclusion of his own marriage. For the eighth time in her life, Eva – now forty-six years old – was pregnant! It was certainly not in vain that the beautiful widow had grown young again to play at «Saltimbanques».

– I live in you, that truly has a double meaning now, wrote Eva to the insanely happy Honoré. He no longer had any doubts about this marriage so deeply desired. And he decreed: it will be a boy, Victor-Honoré. But to Napoleón, his paragon, Victor Hugo replied with this mysterious whisper:

> *Non, l'avenir n'est à personne!*
> *Sire, l'avenir est à Dieu...*

And yet, Eva did not yet make her decision. She abandoned Honoré, who had gathered all the papers necessary for a secret celebration of their marriage in Metz or in Germany, instead of having a big, complicated production, and she accompanied her daughter on the honeymoon... Not until 1847 did she finally decide to go Paris to see the house bought at the price of gold and decorated with so much loving attention. Here a miscarriage delivered her of the fruit of her womb. It was a girl...

Honoré was overcome with grief. Mme Hanska, in whom one senses the relief of being able to procrastinate even more, obliged the stricken writer to accompany her to Forbach. She refused to make any promise or to set any date. She finished by saying that she would return to Ukraine.

—I must put my affairs in order, she claimed, resorting to her usual pretext.

How little she seemed to be attracted by the prospect of this marriage! Was it physical aversion? Hardly. Instead, it was fear of self-degradation, fear of the prejudices of her milieu, fear also of her family who could so easily cast her off.

This last blow felled our poor Balzac. He could no longer take up his work again with renewed fervor; the destruction of his paternal hopes crushed him more than any debt. His publishers began to worry as much as his doctor. He had just finished his *Parents pauvres,* which formed a group with *Cousin Pons* and *Cousine Bette.* His colleagues who hastened to declare him «finished» probably felt in the book the brilliant farewell of genius. Had the Napoleón of Letters met his Waterloo?

He was head-high in unpaid bills and compulsory agricultural labor; he again left for Ukraine. «Come,» she had written to him whom he now called his «Predilecta.»

If she warded off the husband, she could ask nothing better than to welcome a lover. The robust embrace of her French *moujik* did not at all repulse the sedate, discreet Slav. Balzac loved the estate which furnished so striking a setting for his mistress; what a site, that immense field of wheat against the dark forest, where in the dead of winter the wolves howled! He marveled at the way the servants bowed before him; he would make sure to speak of this to Zulma Carraud! The luxury of the château transported him: no more creditors here, no more financial worries! The library was at his disposition, as were the set of silverware with its beautifully engraved initials and the antique bathtub. He drank his tea in the finest translucent porcelain from Peking; he fingered books with valuable bindings, donned the skins of bears and foxes killed by faithful Cossacks, manipulated the playing cards on a table of wood from the Islands, beneath a portrait of Maria Leczinska, great-grandmother of his fiancée. For his outings in the forest or over the fields traversed by a narrow path, he rode in a tilbury drawn by two throughbred horses. A bearded valet brought him his coffee in bed every morning. In the midst of these heavenly pleasures, he completed his most devout work, *L'Initié*.

On his departure, Eva covered his shoulders with a magnificent fur coat and showered him with kisses and tender words. But of marriage, not a word! Unbeknownst to him, his beloved had intercepted, with her own dainty white hands, the letter he had written in December to the Czar of Russia, asking him for the hand of his faithful subject...

In Paris once again, Balzac encountered full-scale revolution. The bourgeois king, having entered through one barricade, now in 1848 made his exit through another. Under the name of M. and Mme Lebrun, he and Queen Amélie hid in a hotel before leaving France. But there would be no more Varennes; no one stopped the umbrella-king at the border.

Gautier closed his windows to the storm and in his ivory tower wrote his most famous poems: *Emaux et Camées*. During this time, the discomfitted lover of the lofty Polish lady descended into the Tuileries with the people!

Had he suddenly become a Republican?

Not at all; he had merely yielded to his curiosity, wishing to see the place where the kings lived. Among the crowd was Flaubert accompanied by Maxime du Camp, but Balzac did not know them. On the other hand, he was only too well acquainted with Emile de Kirardin, the husband of Delphine Gay, named «the Corsaire of Letters» with whom he had tangled heatedly. Meanwhile, George Sand smoked her cigar beneath the marble arcades, kissed Lamartine, and caused a great fuss.

In the midst of such turbulence the oratorical clubs flourished. One of them, «the Universal Brotherhood,» showed itself willing to inscribe Balzac's name on a list of Republican candidates; but Honoré proudly refused:

— The Republic, that is our malady!

It was his way of remaining faithful to the poor dead Laure whom he had so often deceived, while she was alive, with rivals of flesh and blood.

At home again, he lashed at his imagination, straining to find his Pegasus which seemed to have shrunk to the level of a hired horse. The «Family Museum» bought his story, *L'Initié,* at a low price. Indifferent to the hue and cry of the Republicans, Balzac continued his mad acquisitions for the home in the rue Fortunée.

The walls must be hung with gold damask, the doors chiseled in ivory, the stairway covered with fine rugs. Nick-nacks, mirrors, twisted candle-holders piled up everyhere. Nothing was too beautiful for the Northern Star! Ever since «Noré» had been with his beloved among her treasures and her prostrate servants, wearing her sable cloak and carrying a hunting whip in her hand, he had measured the distance separating them and strived to render this cage acceptable to a lovely Czarina. To the very last inch of floor and wall, the palace was ready... The fairy had only to come; nothing else was missing.

Balzac's mother, furious about his expenses, quarrelled violently with her son, who called her «a monster, a monstrosity.» This opinion was upheld by the doctor called in for consultation: «Why no, she is not crazy, she is simply mean...» The old woman was indignant about the outrageous disdain exhibited towards her by Mme Hanska; never a line inquiring about her, or about any other nember of this common family; one would say she was preparing to marry an orphan! Was she only preparing? What excuse could she present as a screen? None; she could not admit that she trembled at the idea of entering a family of vinegrowers and lace-makers!

The moutain could not go to Mohammed, so Mohammed went to the mountain; Honoré returned again to Ukraine! Truly this man, so tired and overworked, had an undying hope. But this time, the atmosphere between the lovers was spoiled. Mme Hanska, who had contributed some of her wealth to the acquisition of the Beaujon mansion – they had even nicknamed their strong-box «loulou» – exploded in anger on learning of the enormity of the expenditures. Heated arguments followed.

Balzac could no longer dissemble the truth. He admitted:

«– Here she is rich, loved, esteemed, and it costs her nothing; she hesitates to go to a place where she sees nothing but troubles, debts, and new faces.

Who would have believed it? And yet, it was at that very time that the marriage was definitely settled; thanks, however, to a forbidding event: Balzac's illness, whose tragic end was clearly seen by the doctors.

«– I am as thin as I was in 1819, sighed Balzac. The disease turns me into a child...

The ruined organism foundered at last. It was the moment long foreseen by Doctor Nacquart.

Eva called upon two eminent physicians, the father and son Knothe. Their treatment consisted... of lemon juice; resulting in nothing but violent stomach aches. Mme Hanska and her daughter Anna were quite vexed, for they had promised themselves a share in the lively social season in Kiev, dancing and exhibiting their clothing and their jewels. Such ladies do not shine with abnegation. Balzac bitterly wrote to his old confidante Zulma, whom he had disgracefully neglected in recent years:

«With what rapidity does misfortune hatch, and how many obstacles

An astounding consumption of gloves! Fifty-eight pair in two months! In this absurd and capricious fancy for food and worthless objects, in this anxiety to appear rich and noble, or to feel that way, a psycho-analyst would probably see the frustration born of a childhood deprived of maternal love.

bar the way to happiness... For three years I built a nest which cost a fortune, and alas, the birds are missing...»

He seemed ready to renounce this mirage devoid of both rhyme and reason, this marriage promised in 1833 by a Polish Bovary to a romantic young man out to assault the world. But the doctors had probably forewarned Mme Hanska. As soon as she knew him beyond hope, nothing further prevented the union which, in her mind, would soon give way to glorious widowhood.

The thing was concluded: Balzac seemed to recover. To his old mother playing dragon for a den of treasure, he sent a letter filled with minute household details, a long list of orders such as a servant might receive: a certain Japanese vase must be arranged with a certain flower, the objects must be disposed in a certain way, etc. Later, he sent an even more surprising missive, written in a very embarassed style for he was all too conscious of his odious attitude; he did not wish his mother to be there on their arrival. What pretext could he employ to humor his mother's conceit, to avoid an affront because her daughter-in-law did not think her worthy enough to kiss her slippers? It was quite simple: Mme Balzac's dignity risked being compromised by the unpacking! It was to his sister Laure that he sent the letter, a masterpiece of dishonesty in which one senses Mme Hanska's ultimatum.

At Berdichev, on March 14, the marriage was celebrated in the little church of St. Barbara, in the strictest intimacy. Balzac was so ill that he feared he could not drag himself to the altar, and he said to his eternal fiancée:

—I shall be dead before I marry you!

They then had to await the thaw. Bandits were ravaging the countryside, a fortunate delay for Balzac whose condition would be gravely endangered by a trip at this time; he had just had another heart attack. The journey from the estate to the Polish border took six days; the couple required a month. When they were ready to leave the land of Ukraine, Balzac was half blind and incapable even of climbing a step. Would he ever see the soil of France again?

In Dresden he wrote his letters, although his eyes refused to function and his swollen fingers painfully descended the length of the page. Meanwhile, Mme Eva de Balzac went off to buy herself a necklace worth five hundred dollars, which she then described with unfaltering hand in a letter, as Balzac scrawled his last lies to his mother: if Eva did not write to her it was because her rheumatism of the joints prevented her from tracing a single line.

Honoré's servant, François, had also received his list of precise instructions: he was to light the chandeliers and be prepared to welcome them, a garland of flowers in his hand. One would say a ruler, a royal princess that the impotent author now led to the rue Fortunée.

The last stage of the journey was completed by railroad; and then a hackney-cab to bring the couple to the doorstep. But now, as in one of Balzac's novels, the return so scrupulously planned and so dearly paid was heralded by an unforeseen and dramatic event. In front of the brilliantly lighted windows, the sick man knocked loudly on the door and received no answer; a locksmith had to be called to break into his own house while Mme de Balzac waited, haughty and impatient. The mother was not there, in accordance with the orders of her son. However, instead of being on the threshold with garlands of flowers, François had gone stark-raving mad and was rolling on the armchairs of the salon; they had to force him into a strait-jacket.

Could one have imagined a more gripping and romantic event? What incredible occurrence, what presentiment could have brought on the madness of this mild-tempered servant? Had the display of candelabra and torches which he so dutifully lighted served to reinforce, in its more colossal proportions, the shadow of Falsehood looming behind the master of the house?

«When the household lies in readiness,» says a Turkish proverb, «it is death that enters in.»

It was a beautiful May evening of 1850; Balzac had just turned fifty-one. In August he would die, after sixteen years of correspondence and little more than a year of life with the proud Eva.

Flaubert was aghast before such a curse:

«This end is atrocious,» he wrote. «To be so stricken in the fullness of conjugal happiness!»

But could one really speak of happiness? At the cost of outlandish and ridiculous efforts, Balzac had met failure on the threshold of all he had ever desired on earth and could not obtain, save by that very failure. Would Mme Hanska have married him if he had not been condemned to die? Certainly not; her entire conduct proves that.

A great *voluntarist* who would have appealed to Balzac, Arthur Rimbaud, knew the same lavish determination and the same striking disavowal of fortune. Of what consequence the mutilated pioneer's belt filled with gold, or the wedding ring of the successful man stricken in the arms of his muse! Death does not cheat. He changes men only in themselves.

Balzac's conjugal happiness was nothing but a façade. He lived now in complete material security, for the first time since he had been writing — but he could no longer write. He had married the woman he loved – but he could not make love with her, he could barely speak to her, and benefit from her company. The doctors forbade him the effort of talking. The rooms had been decorated to his taste, but no one came to visit him; the library overflowed with costly books, and he could not even read a single page. At the table where he could hardly manage to eat, or in his vast bed, alone and moaning, everywhere the writer awaited the end of his suffering. Not by the side of a Laure or a Zulma who would have been angelic nurses, but in the hands of a cold, birdlike woman who considered the tragedy nothing but an annoying duty, fortunately drawing to its end.

Four French doctors, among them Nacquart, could only confirm the hopeless diagnosis of their colleagues in Ukraine. His mother, once so selfish with the child and then the young man, now came with reborn kindness to sit by the side of the sick man who had had so little place in her life. Undoubtedly, no great politeness was lost between the mother and her daughter-in-law.

The night of the 17 and 18 of August, the agony began. Legend has it that from the depths of his delirium, Balzac called one last time:

–Bianchon! Send me Bianchon! *He* will save me!

Bianchon, the famous doctor of *La Comédie humaine,* supposedly inspired by Doctor Blanche, was now summoned to the bedside of his creator! *Si non è vero!* Nothing was more in keeping with the character and entire life of Balzac than the little incident that transpired one day as he sat writing: A knock on his door was followed by a voice announcing in jest: «It's Eugénie Grandet» Without raising his head, Balzac answered: «Good, very good, come in!»

Victor Hugo was present during his final moments, which he later described with extreme gravity and force. He told of the terrible solitude of the dying author, unconscious, and gasping for breath, his head rolling from side to side in an obscurity pierced by the light of torches. Only a servant girl cried... Mme de Balzac was not in the room. Furious about this neglect, commentators have suggested that she was at the same moment delivering herself up to the hideous painter Gigoux, her future husband. But that is nothing more than legend. It is useless to blacken the tableau; one need only know the selfishness and fickleness of this woman devoid of grandeur. «All that is exaggerated is weak,» said Talleyrand.

When the time came to arrange for the funeral, his wife gave proof of the slight interest she had taken in her husband's social life. As pallbearers she chose the minister Baroche, hardly Balzac's intimate, whom the writer called «that eminent man!»; then Alexandre Dumas, who had sided against the deceased in a lawsuit with the publisher Buloz; Sainte-Beuve, the only writer for whom Balzac had evinced throughout his whole life a furious hostility! The fourth, Victor Hugo, was the only suitable party.

The latter saved the situation by uttering a splendid funeral oration. To the followers of the cortège who only half listened as they kicked the dust of August, he dared to say:

«Unknown to him, whether he wished it or not, the author of this immortal work belongs to the mighty race of revolutionary writers.»

After his death, the magnificent mansion of the rue Fortunée, left to the widow for whom it had been so lovingly and painstakingly prepared, was totally neglected. She now set up house with Gigoux, a mediocre painter of such ugliness that he had been nicknamed «the louse». Estranged from the Balzac family, she then brought action against Alexandre Dumas who, despite his past attitude, had wanted to erect a monument to Balzac. After squandering her fortune and the royalties from *La Comédie humaine,* Balzac's widow died in miserable conditions.

The last memorable words of Balzac had been:

«—I am part of the opposition which is called life.

The case of Honoré de Balzac is unique in French literature, and for more than one reason. Like Proust, he had a host of imitators and not one disciple; he couldn't possibly.

In the words of Albert Thibaudet:

«*La Comédie humaine* is the witness and living museum of a French century.

«Actually, it contains more than the century; its roots extend to the generation of 1789, to the French Revolution, and particularly to the history of Balzac's generation which was twenty years old in 1820, and encountered its great division in 1850, the year of Balzac's death. But it was a division for men, not for events, for Balzac, and not for the living comedy of his time.

»It has been commented several times that *La Comédie humaine* predicted and pre-formed the society of the Second Empire. The generation of 1850 was a Balzachian generation. And Balzac continued to instruct, penetrate and magnetize the generation of 1885 France. The Balzachian world and the nineteenth century, which began in 1789, ended in 1914. With the generation of 1914, *La Comédie humaine* assumed the shape of a novel or historic cycle.»

Not very well known, this judgment is of great importance. Even more important is the comment of Frederick Engels who wrote, in 1888:

«I have learned more (from Balzac) than in all the books of the historians, economists, and professional statisticians of the epoch taken together.

»In politics, Balzac was very likely a legitimist. His great work is an undying elegy which deplores the irremediable decomposition of the nobility; his sympathies lie with the class condemned to death.

»And yet, in spite of all this, never was his satire more trenchant nor his irony more bitter than when he created his aristocrats, the same men and women for whom he felt such sympathy. Except for a few provincials, the only men of whom he spoke with undisguised admiration were his most avid political adversaries, the fiery Republican heroes of the Saint-Merri cloister, who represented, in this epoch (1830-1860), the true masses of the people.» (Letter to Miss Harkness.)

This view, which restates the opinión uttered by Victor Hugo in the cemetery, also recalls the observation of a librarian, Charles Weiss, whom Balzac had met during his first trip to Neuchâtel:

«In politics, Balzac calls himself a legitimist, and he speaks like a liberal. My conclusion is that he himself does not know very well what he thinks!»

This split between the underlying temperament and the opinion expressed in all honesty was already a rare thing in France. Was it an absence of lucidity? It is evident that Balzac did not manifest any clarity of thought when he attempted to reason, and that on the other hand, he reached unimagined depths with the power of his vision and the keeness of his intuition. About himself, he was mistaken all his life. He constantly saw himself on the verge of realizing his most precious hopes, of making his fortune, of grasping that which was just beyond his reach and which would escape him forever. Rare were his moments of clairvoyance, such as the one in 1834 which caused him to sigh:

«It is said that I shall never have full happiness, liberation, liberty... save in perspective.»

And in 1847, during one of those depressions that announced the end of his creative force much more than the commencement of a harsh lucidity:

«I am left with neither heart nor soul; everything has died... I shall die exhausted, of work and anxiety... My weariness is incurable... I am getting thinner, I am interested in nothing... I lose myself more and more in the unending idleness of melancholy. I am unconscious of life; I no longer believe in the future.» He then had only three more years of life.

In the depths of despair, this reproach:

«Work, dear author of *La Comédie humaine*. Pay for your luxury, atone for your follies, and await your Eva in the hell of your ink-stand and white paper!»

Occasionally, the author of this immense fresco succeeded in evaluating the Pascalian vanity of the things of this world, at whose altar he so frequently served as fervent and covetous celebrant.

Nevertheless, it was extremely rare to find, in his day and age, a French writer crowned by the approbation of the elite as well as of the masses; the few to whom this good fortune has arrived belonged to the nineteenth century. Sand, Hugo and Balzac passed to posterity with different honors. In France, the authors disposing of huge royalties and a large public are, with few exceptions, scorned by «the scholars.» The writers extolled by this latter group are those completely ignored by the public and unsupported by substantial royalties, or at least during their lifetime. It is the phenomenon of the «accursed poet» which, since the time of *Chatterton* (the English bard frenchified by Vigny and so irritating to Balzac) down to Nerval, Rimbaud and Lautréamont, runs like a dark filigree through the golden Book of Letters.

Another trait isolates Balzac on his island of success. In France, it is by his style that a writer preserves his face before posterity; the form of psychology and the interest stemming from the plot are relegated to second place, or rather remain inseparable, owing to the particularity of the language for a certain beauty of expression. In England, the same requirement does not exist. Dickens, with his brisk sabottage of the English tongue, knew the very same success with the elite and the masses, to whom his wonderfully alive characters appealed enormously. The English language, like the German, possesses a fluidity rendering it infinitely more suited to the deformations characteristic of the romantic temperament. French is much more codified and algebraic, making it much more difficult for a writer to take liberties. Balzac, however, succeeded.

With every line, in fact, he outraged the most sacrosant rules of their literary tradition. It was not a question of offending the «clarity» and «measure» whose praises were sung in scholarly manuals in a very scholastic tone that did not, in any case, prevent an Aubigné or a Lautréamont from writing a work of genius in French. Instead, with Balzac it was more a matter of deliberate departure from the meaning of the language. His prose suffered from turgidness as his body from obesity; he produced one hundred words in the place of one, not for the purpose of slowly developing the meaning as in Proust, but because he failed to strike the right term on the first blow; thus he displayed it with all the others, like the priceless object mingled with the cheap wares in a Persian market. His verbal acrobatics grew even more

35

striking, his contrasts more naïve; and instead of gliding subtly through certain thoughts he insisted on emphasizing them like a nouveau-riche crying out the price of the jewel he wears. He was not satisfied with the depiction of the père Goriot as a truly sublime figure; he must proceed to announce it to the reader: «Goriot is sublime!» Swinburne called it «the smell of grease,» and the great English poet adds that Balzac forgot to clean the corners of his novel. Never, and with no writer, have the French scholars and their posterity pardoned such faults. Victim of his own wonder before the splendor of a gaping mind, the coarse fellow forgot a certain fundamental refinement and so jolted the ink-well with his pachydermic gambols that he has left us spattered with spots. Must the swarming fresco remain prodigious in order that our mandarin-like sensibility, exacerbated by an old cultural tradition, forgive Balzac so flagrant a scorn of decorum!

By the same candor, the good Honoré could not help but be in absolute contradiction with himself. The world as he described it so vividly was a crying negation of all his dearest theories on order, religion, the sanctity of autocratic and aristocratic power, morality based on property, etc., etc.

The personal choices of Balzac in politics and theology had as much of a connection with what he revealed to us under his entomologist's lense, as the Balzac of one of his novels, speaking judiciously on the enormous value of Holbein, had with the Balzac who, for sixty dollars, thought he had acquired an authentic Holbein for his mansion!

When he mixed with life instead of literature, Balzac gave the appearance of a print-maker whose fingers still retain some of the gold paint from his work, and everything that he touches, even the most trivial of things, begins to glimmer.

Certain critics like Murciaux have said that he was a firm royalist in thought but that a secret stirring in his entrails carried him toward the interests of the common people from whom he had issued. This is not so. He never displayed the slightest trace of that which in the case of Hugo and Sand was high-minded indignation. From such as these, he defended in all good conscience the beauties of obscurantism. In Ukraine he was enchanted by the reverences that would have horridly embarassed even the most timid of liberals. In other words, he is unknowingly, «of the mighty race of revolutionary writers» simply because the rigorous, scientific honesty of his craft reveals things as they are. In this he was highly advanced, precisely because the ignorance of his self-contradiction enabled him to probe much more deeply than the confirmed socialists like Hugo and Sand, whose philosophy sprang from *sentiment*; thus, they thought above all of saying what they believed to be true, instead of revealing the objective exterior. When they thought they were exposing a situation, they were only lavishing pity on misfortune. With the impassiveness of a man of science, Balzac took apart the mechanism.

At an elegant dinner or reception, where the guests wished to hear speeches on art and literature, Balzac would describe at length, amid general annoyance and disturbance, the various combinations he constructed to best exploit his work. No wonder the sophisticated judged him crude and vulgar; he dared to say out loud what one did, but never spoke of! Flaubert himself, in his letters, displays his astonishment. What little love for the beautiful, and what a love of money, he thought. But Balzac was talking here like a man of means; of small means, certainly, for he had renounced almost every human pleasure in his heroic passion for literature; but of means nonetheless, who had no need to sell in order to know his «image».

This practical, concrete manner of revealing the situation involved another advantage which could impose silence on the sticklers for refinement. Trapped in his condition with very little capital in a century when capitalism was triumphant, Balzac was the first writer to define and lay the basis for a new jurisdiction on literary ownership. One must not forget that at this time, no legislation protected the work of an author; Belgian bookstores and printing-shops, for example, could publish a French work without handing over a cent of the copywrite privileges. Balzac was a founder of the Société des Gens de Lettres. Going always to the extremity of an idea, he even attempted to form a freemasonry of writers who would assist each other in all places and circumstances (and immediately his wild imagination conjured up the most bizarre places and the most adventurous situations). «For Balzac, the future does not exist, evarything lies in the present,» wrote Théophile Gautier, in his description of Balzac's efforts and of the charm he exerted over his colleagues. When they gathered – after only four times – he founded and baptized *The Red Horse*.

Thus, without specific mention, the political aspect is present in *La Comédie humaine,* as the Jewish question unspokenly pervades the work of Kafka. Humanity here is described in terms of the Darwinian jungle where reings the law of maximal profit; which is all the more reason for Engels to admire the penetration of Balzac. Since the last century, anyone who does some economy also does politics. Therefore it is surprising to note that the critic, Bernard Guyon, in his *Centenary Book* dedicated to Balzac, reproaches him for not dealing with political questions, when it is evident that he is one of the most political of the great nineteenth-century writers – which is not to intend «politician» or even «engagé.»

The second, more modern aspect of this colossal work, flowing directly from the first, is Balzac's existential amorality. In spite of his abundant declamations, there is never a «moral judgment» in the descriptive work of Balzac. Already, for Flaubert the most precious quality of a writer lay in what can be called «the withdrawal.» «God did not leave a judgment on his work; how then could I utter one?» he would say to those who grew impatient over his lack of ethical conclusions. While the lesser novelist accorded himself a moral statement, Balzac was content to call upon a more scientific method. It was for this reason that the Catholic, conformist Honoré de Balzac could calmly speak about a thief in terms of a particularly formidable species, or a very efficacious poisonous plant. In stripping this nineteenth-century theme a little bit, we find «Milord l'Arsouille,» the bad, but so well-brought-up son of Eugène Sue; then, the convict of Rimbaud, «sole witness of his reason and his glory.» Paris, at this time, saw the proliferation of the dangerous classes: delinquents, house-breakers, assassins – these are the direct descendents of the motley crew constituting the «rolling army» in which served Vidocq. The police, in turn, branched out and became corrupted, as well as more effective; from simple militia destined to protect the bourgeois, they served as counter-offensive for the cohorts in crime, employing their methods and resorting to the infiltrations of indicators, the creation of Fouché. Before this spectacle, so exciting to the romantic imagination, André Maurois has reason to observe: «Balzac sincerely praises a tiger.» In our day, Genêt would add to the same process an entire scheme of erotic dynamism; that of Balzac was uniquely one of effectiveness, so dear to a mercantile, industrial century.

But did this world so closely observed, this century so minutely analysed, correspond to his model? Was Balzac a good photograph or an impressionistic visionary? Did the world of *La Comédie humaine* exist beyond his imagination?

We must not hesitate to give the answer: The exterior world in which he lived, and which he attempted to describe, was a world *transposed.*

Do we not, in the art of painting, attain a truth superior to that of photography which only seizes the surface and petrifies the moment which is restored in a true painting?

Levaillant has quite accurately called Balzac «a visionary of the real.» The terms are not contradictory. It is not of a naturalist that he spoke. In Balzac's own words on the subject:

«Try to shape the hand of your mistress and to pose it before you; you will find a horrible cadaver bearing no resemblance to the real thing; you must then go in search of the man who, without making an exact copy, will seize the movement and the life.»

Balzac adheres to the dialectic logic of the world when he integrates movement and becoming with life itself. Suspended life is not life, but the image of death.

The preceding gives a general idea of the still vital actuality of Balzac; but it would be neither right nor honest to avoid a consideration of the opposite element in *La Comédie humaine,* its veritable inactuality.

In the western world of the twentieth century, the modalities have changed, perhaps, but the base, beneath the immense surface of variation, is the same: political economy. The striking inactuality of the work does not derive from the evolution of the subject ─ society ─ but from the methods used to describe it.

In the course of a discussion on the «Balzac subject», a great contemporary writer affirmed that the reality which offers itself to our efforts today, being much more complex than that of the nineteenth century, cannot be approached with the same instruments used by our predecessors. To deal with a problem of matter after the days of Planck and Lord Rutherford, could we possibly use Pasteur's microscope? All genius of observation is inevitably surpassed, not by the genius of the following generation, but by the perfection of methods acquired in the course of the technical development. One can say as much abut writers of the same century, like Dostoievsky or Stendhal; but if the emphasis of obsoleteness is laid on Balzac, it is because the partisans of the «traditional novel» refer more readily to him than to the others. As soon as an author sets down a character defined by social relations, he is branded a Balzachian! It is thought that an epoch which refers increasingly to «totality» has need of something else.

But be careful, says another analyst, Michel Butor:

«It is child's play to show that this *actual* novel à la Balzac was inspired much more by an infinitely small part of Balzac's work.»

In fact, the modern French emulator of Balzac will dwell on *Le Père Goriot* or *Eugénie Grandet* or on all the other more or less well-known works, rather than steep himself in the totality of *La Comédie humaine.*

Michel Butor draws an accurate conclusion from this state of affairs:

«If one takes any novel from those that compose *La Comédie humaine,* it is rather easy to reveal the elements that oppose it to present literature, making it out-dated; but if one takes the work in its entirety, one discovers that its richness and audacity have, until the present, been far from appreciated for their true value.»

We thus arrive at the following conclusion, which may seem paradoxical:

The best followers of Balzac today are perhaps those who seem most remote from him. In the same way that Picasso, who is capable of drawing a bull like Rubens, seems to turn his back on the latter much more radically than a lesser academic painter. And so those who, like new wine, have made the old bottles of the novel sparkle: Joyce, Proust, Faulkner, Butor (much more so than the «traditionals» and «Balzachians») are the sons of this tremendous fighter, this Gulliver of Letters, forever in his dressing-gown ready to do battle with the angel, bending his shoulders to his century, that he might keep on the pages of his work the monumental mark of the giant he had conquered.

Bernard-François Balssa (and not Balzac), the author's father. A commoner of Albigensian peasant-stock who had received only a few lessons from the village notary and then made his fortune in the Revolution, he had a son who dreamed of nobility and added the aristocratic *de* to his name.

Tours and the Loire at the time of the writer's birth. «Do not ask me why I love Touraine,» he later said, «I love it as an artist loves art.»

The Collège des Oratoriens of Vendôme (as seen today), where ▶ the young Honoré was placed at the age of eight. In *Louis Lambert*, Balzac evokes his unhappy memories of this gloomy boarding-school in which he spent six years of childhood.

His sister Laure, one year younger than he, was his confidante and friend.

Anne Charlotte Laure Sallambier, his mother, in a water-color in the «House of Balzac.» The implacable obstinacy of eye, sharp and lucid, the chin imperceptibly accentuated by a thin layer of flesh, tracing even then the future shrew.

The school and its various buildings, in a lithograph at the National Library. More of a design than an actual image, it seems better suited to a fortress or a barracks. With its grass plots, its winding paths, its façades of long, narrow openings, its angles and parallels, it seemed a well-planned trap.

The lawyer, Guillonnet de Merville, in whose practice Balzac served temporarily as clerk, filling everyone's ears with inexhaustible stories. Later, when Balzac had become famous, the lawyer remembered his former «partner» and treated him every year to a sumptuous dinner.

The young man Balzac lodged for a while in this house in the rue Tournefort, Paris. With his two chairs, his little oak table, his bed no wider than a board, and a linen closet which he had papered himself, he heroically held siege against the natural enemies of poverty: hunger, cold, and fatigue.

The playground, in a print of the time. «It was very difficult for him to adapt to the regulations of the institution,» say his biographers. His health was so gravely affected there that his family withdrew him in April 1813.

The boisterous clerk often lived in a world of his own. «He would resemble,» writes his sister Laure, «those somnambulists who sleep with their eyes open; he would not hear most of the questions addressed to him.»

Mme de Berny, in a portrait by Van Gorp. Twenty years
Balzac's senior, she was his generous mistress, a friend in
difficult times, encouraging him and assisting him financially.
She inspired his unforgettable Mme de Mortsauf in *Le Lys
dans la Vallée*.

A view of the Place de la Concorde in Balzac's youth. The meager allowance given him by his father hardly permitted him to discover Paris: «During this long period of work I do not remember having crossed the Pont des Arts (that is, having crossed the Seine from the left bank to the right), nor ever having bought water; I would get some in the morning from the fountain on the Place Saint Michel» (near the rue Tournefort).

In 1825, Balzac set up a publishing house, but the business soon went into deficit. In an attempt to save it he added on a printing shop at 17, rue des Marais-Saint-Germain – today the rue Visconti, one of the narrowest streets in Old Paris.

The entrance of the printing shop, rue des Marais-Saint-Germain. The building replaced a former garden through which, according to Tallemant des Réaux, the nobleman Vauquelin des Yvetaux received Ninos de Lenclos and many other fair ladies. On the opposite side of the street is the house in which Racine and Adrienne Lecouvreur died. Several famous actresses also lived along this street: Champmeslé, Clairon.

Like Venus visiting Vulcan in his cavern, Laure de Berny would often bring her charming presence to brighten the dark hovel where the young novelist, launched headlong into the world of business, struggled in full disarray. Sustained by the lunch and the encouragement she brought him, he would then permit himself a walk in the Luxembourg gardens, or a drink with his friend Thomassey in the Café Voltaire, as he outlined sublime projects.

When the business was in danger of bankruptcy, Mme de Berny bought the printing shop and entrusted its management to her son Alexander, having him declared of age although he was only nineteen. Despite his youth he directed with a skillful hand and later, in association with Laurent, he assured so successful a future for the enterprise that it continued its activities to the present day. It was the famous House of Deberny and Peignot.

The Duchess of Abrantès was fifteen years older than Balzac. Unable to exert the same attraction after forty as did Laure de Berny, she nevertheless still possessed a great deal of vivacity and wit, as well as a beautiful home in the rue de Montreuil. She could assume all the elegant grace she wore when, with a necklace of twelve thousand dollars about her neck, she throned among the dignitaries of Malmaison, never very far from Napoleon.

Balzac settled in the rue Cassini, a section of nondescript homes, gardens, and road-side inns, where he rented the entire floor of a shaded house, furnishing it on credit. In this stylish apartment – bookcase with mahogany shelves, Jouy tapestry, soft rugs, a clock of yellow marble with gold inlay, books bound in red Maroccan leather – his full stomach at ease in a long monk's robe, the strange young man of twenty-nine awaited inspiration. To his mother who clamored: «His debts are growing!», he answered: «My credit is growing.»

Lively, supple, easy of temper, passionate of heart, irreproachable in virtue, highly cultivated and critical of mind, his friend Zulma Carraud stood way above her circle of relations. She welcomed with delight the apparition in her claustrophobic life of this big, coarse, boisterous fellow, radiating heartiness and genius. All her life, her lucid affection followed the author of *La Comédie humaine*.

And Balzac wrote to her, «I have for you an affection which resembles no other, and it will have neither rival nor parallel.»

For Balzac the eyes of Mme d'Abrantès possessed the fabulous merit of having reflected Napoleon ensconced in his glory, of having seen him «concerned with the details of life, then ... grow, magnify, and cover the world with his name!»

A portrait of Princess Bagration in whose home Balzac met the aristocracy, the cream of the Faubourg Saint-Honoré. «You would like to know if I have met Fédora, if she is real?» would say Balzac. «A woman from the cold plains of Russia, the princess Bagration, comes to Paris to be its paragon.»

The state «la Grenadière» in Touraine, the county-seat in *Le Lys dans la Vallée* which he described in his inimitable way: «It lies in the heart of Touraine, that charming little Touraine where all the flowers, fruits and beauties of the region are fully represented...» Until his death, Balzac would regret the rolling countryside of Touraine with its charm and agreeable climate, only one aspect of the sweetness of life which was almost never his to taste.

The beautiful semi-invalid, Mme de Castries, who inspired the *Duchesse de Langeais*. Daughter of the Duke of Maillé and wife of the Marquis of Castries, her beauty had been renowned and her life tumultuous. In former times she made a striking figure in the salons of the Duchess de Berry, with her crown of golden tresses like Ceres' diadem and her gown of nacarat flowing from her magnificent shoulders.

Balzac's room at «la Mimerolle,» the estate in the Saumur region where the novelist had come to gather information before writing *Eugénie Grandet,* the most popular book of *La Comédie humaine.*
The main character may very well have been inspired by Jean Nivelleau, a wealthy usurer who lived not far from Saché, where the Margonne family received Balzac. His daughter's beauty was famous in the area and his nephew claimed that Balzac wrote *Eugénie Grandet* to avenge himself for having been dismissed as an imposter.

◀ A view of the Loire at Tours. For those who know the river today, so often sandy and shallow, it is difficult to imagine that only last century it was travelled by many boats and that Balzac and Mme de Berny were able to take a cruise on its waters.

During his more prosperous years, Balzac would often go to the «Café de Paris» on the corner of the rue Taitbout. The establishment was reputed for «its Ostende oysters, its cutlets Soubise, its chicken Marengo, its mushroom pies soaked in bordeaux, liqueurs and champagne.»

Balzac carried, not by «thirty year old women» as the inscription often read, but by women «who were thirty years old ten years ago,» according to the caption of this caricature drawn from *La Grande Course au Clocher académique.*

Balzac was extremely proud of his canes. This one, with golden handle, was about three feet long. The golden chain of turquoise was given to him during his stay in Geneva, by Mme Hanska.

The writer possessed several others, equally famous: one whose copper handle represented the head of a mastiff, another on whose sculpted ivory head a lion and a lioness kissed, two more with monkeys on silver handles.

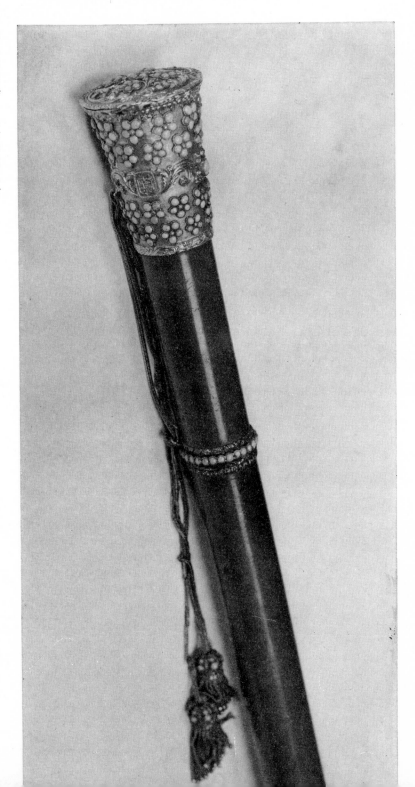

The Countess Hanska, the mysterious reader who wrote to him from the confines of Europe. Wife of an enormously wealthy man, she had no other distractions but to devour foreign novels, to beget children and watch them die; such was the faraway person who stifled of boredom on her pile of gold and found nothing better to fill her time than the mystification of the Parisian author in vogue.

After four sleepless nights, with a new horse at every post, he arrived in Neuchâtel on September 25, 1833, overcome with fatigue and impatience. A letter from Mme Hanska had fixed an encounter on the promenade between one and four o'clock. There he met the unknown goddess, the northern star, the Stranger, the Chosen One!

The «harbor» at Neuchâtel, in the nineteenth century, as seen by Mme Hanska and Balzac.

«If I had the right to desire what is reserved only for the rich,» wrote Balzac to Mme Hanska, «I would spend my honeymoon at Diodati, perhaps even making it my customary residence.»

The Villa Diodati in Geneva, where Byron and Shelley stayed.

Born beneath the sign of the Bull, Balzac had its physical aspects: a thick-set body, a brief look betokening a gathered force ready to be unleashed, flat, broad facial features, a sanguine complexion, large mane of hair. But it was his character, above all, that corresponded with his star: tenacity, prodigious energy, willfulness, ponderousness and sensuality.

It was here that he wrote *Le Père Goriot, Louis Lambert,* and many other works. Whether he came to Saché to rest, to flee his creditors, or even to hide, Balzac never ceased to work and to bring his habits there.

A view of the Château de Saché, «admirable in its grace and peace-
fulness,» writes André Maurois.
«They accept me in these parts like a child,» said Balzac. «Here I have
no significance, but I am free and happy to be here.»
There Balzac occasionally consented to read several pages of a novel
he was working on to the guests of his host. The candelabra were
placed around the room and he would go from one to the other, not
only reading his text, but impersonating, inventing, carrying on dial-
ogues, while his bulky shadow moved along the walls in the lamplight

It was in the environs of the village of Saché, in the valley of the Indre, that Balzac set his *Lys dans la Vallée*. Since that time nothing in the surroundings has changed. The little town of Pont-de-Ruan, whose countryside is one of the most cheerful and attractive in Touraine, is perhaps less populated today, but its mills on the riverbank continue to move their huge wooden wheels.

◄ The Château de Valesne (Frapesle in *Le Lys dans la Vallée*), an old Renaissance residence whit mullioned windows and high-roofed wings.
You clamber up a few stone steps and you almost find Mme Mortsauf at her work; on the gravel pathway you can hear the impatient footsteps of her friend; at the end of the path is the garden and then the meadow descending to the stream where they go to gather bouquets of wild flowers.

Sometimes, instead of writing, Balzac doodled. The first drafts ▶ of his works were nothing but illegible scribble, impossible to decipher in their manuscript form. The indignation and complaints of his publishers were ineffectual. The manuscripts continued to be written in hieroglyphics, abbreviations, over-lapping words, rendering the reading a total madness. The proof-readers protested furiously against this maze of scrawl; in vain were they offered an increase in salary, for they refused to «do Balzac.» A special reader must be trained.

Illusions perdues — manuscript page

A view of Milan, in an old engraving. In twenty days «we had to see so many things – Lake Maggiore, Lake Orta, the valley of Sion, Lake Geneva, Vevey, Lausanne, the Valtellina, Bourg and its beautiful church – that we did not have enough time.»

To fulfil a wish of Mme Hanska, Balzac had his portrait done by the painter Boulanger, for which, as he claimed, he abandoned his «modest habits.» Exhibited in the Salon of 1837, the work was not at all liked. The model, however, declared himself satisfied: «That which Boulanger knew how to capture, and of which I am proud, is the persistence of a Coligny, of a Peter the Great, the foundation of my character ... The eyes, especially, are well-rendered, but more in the general psychic expression of the writer than in the loving spirit of the person ...» Two years later he changed his mind: «Boulanger made me look like a trooper and a bully.»

«La Bouleaunnière,» an estate rented by Mme de Berny, near Gretz-sur-Loing, where Balzac wrote part of his *Peau de Chagrin.* The poor *Dilecta,* counselor, friend, mother, first and best of his beloved women, died here in solitude while Balzac went about Italy enjoying life!

Ville-d'Avray in Balzac's time. In the valley of Sèvres he had built an estate, «Les Jardies,» which was to become famous and which still stands today. During its construction the novelist imagined sumptuous – and illusory – decorations on its walls: «Here a wall of Parian marble ... Here a stylobate in cedar wood ... Here a mantelpiece of cipolin marble ... Here a ceiling painted by Delacroix ... Here a mirror of Venetian glass ... Here a painting by Raphael ...,» etc.

◀ «Les Jardies» only added to Balzac's problems. Complaints, arguments, threats of a lawsuit, all of Paris was up in arms over the latest rustic ventures of Monsieur de Balzac!

«The Reverend Father Dom Seraphitus culus Mysticus Goriot, of the common order of Clichy Fathers,» reads this caricature published by the newspaper *Les Ecoles,* calumnizing the writer in danger of arrest in the Clichy prison for his debts. Balzac was able to extract himself from these difficulties and for a while, intended to bring a case against the newspaper. But as soon as the danger vanished, he forgot the calumny.

Balzac receiving his friends at «Les Jardies.» For these rustic occasions they dressed in peasant style. Before a group of astonished colleagues, restraining their laughter at the sight of scrawny trees, he would declare with a serious tone that he wished to find there «all the freshness, shade, heights, and verdure of a Swiss valley,» adding – quite paradoxically – that he was going to cultivate pineapple!

Frédérick Lemaître, the greatest actor of his days. He created the first production of *Vautrin* for the Theatre of the Porte Saint-Martin, and at the première he appeared in the principal role of the Mexican general, combed precisely like the king Louis-Philippe. Among those present was the Duke of Orléans, who hastened to inform his father of the curious coincidence. The following day, the play was prohibited and once again, the unhappy Balzac found himself hopeless and penniless. Scraping and bowing, he went in the company of Victor Hugo to plead his case before the Minister of the Interior – all in vain.

◀ Three silhouettes in an engraving: from left to right, Balzac, Lemaître and Gautier. The friendship with the latter was tempestuous and in 1843, it knew a long estrangement.

Peytel, a provincial notary, had murdered his pregnant ▶ wife, a wealthy Creole, and the valet whom he suspected of being her lover. This shocking affair intrigued Balzac all the more because he had known the accused when they worked together on the newspaper *Le Voleur* (The Thief). With Gavarni he went to plead his friend's case. Thus the two accomplices of *The Thief* met again over an affair of murder

◀ The boulevards and the Theatre of the Porte Saint-Martin, during the last century. The play *Vautrin*, performed there for the first time, was the product of one of Balzac's extraordinary ideas, for which he never lacked. It had struck him to entrust the writing of an act to four friends: Ourliac, Lament-Jan, Belloy and Théophile Gautier. It was impossible to resist the man and his whims, and so the good-natured Gautier, ready to begin, inquired about the play's subject:
«Ah!» exclaimed the inimitable Balzac, «if I must tell you what it's about, we'll never get through with it...»

The Château de Frapesle at Issoudun, home of the Carrauds. In this generous haven, close to his most faithful friend, Balzac always found refuge from his creditors, consolation after an unsuccessful love affair, and rest from exhausting labor. «A place at the table, attentive listeners, a big warm bed in winter, the agreeable shade of a tree in summer, and the freedom to walk around in shirt-sleeves expounding on one's grand projects without shocking anybody.» Wasn't this the inn of happiness?

George Sand found Balzac's company rather «pleasant,» although «verbally, a bit wearisome.» Occasionally they would meet at some dinner, and Helm Floyd relates an anecdote from one such evening:

«George Sand had come with her doctor, who was to accompany her to Nohant. The conversation turned to insanity, its symptoms, and outward manifestations, the doctor claiming he was capable of recognizing a madman on the spot. "Do you see one here?" asked George Sand very seriously. Meanwhile, Balzac continued eating with a vengeance, his tangled mass of hair following the movement of head and arm. "There's one!" declared the doctor, "He can't be mistaken!" George Sand burst into laughter, Balzac did likewise, and after the introductions the doctor was condemned to pay for the dinner.»

A portrait of Balzac corresponding closely to the picture he gave of himself: «At first sight he resembled one of those celebrated canons of Boileau... A closer look revealed the ardent melancholy of a mind that could span the horizon, from one extremity to the other.»

The famous white coffee-pot, bearing his initials in violet, was bought in Limoges, renowned for its fine porcelain.

Mme de Brugeol, «the screech-owl», would keep the fire of the night-lamp alive so that Balzac could always drink his coffee scalding hot.

More than any other personality of his time, Balzac served as victim for the caricaturists, whose humor was sometimes ferocious. His habits, his writer's idiosyncracies, his famous dressing-gown, his frequently chimerical ambitions, his silhouette and his elegant mannerisms furnished abundant material for irony!

In the autumn of 1840, Balzac's furniture was seized, and so he rented a house surrounded by trees and shrubs, 19 rue Basse, Passy. Situated on the side of a slope, it was enhanced by a little garden which the novelist enjoyed immensely. Frequently he would install himself there to write, or even to take his bath in a tub. Passy was then praised for its salubrity, the purity of its air, its closeness to the Bois de Boulogne «which make it,» said a chronicler of the time, «one of the most agreeable spots in the Paris region...»

A second doorway enabled Balzac to escape ▶ discreetly from his creditors. At right, an unpublished photograph of the staircase, in the rue Basse, as it was when Balzac knew it.

The study in the house at Passy. For seven years i was the setting of his days and sometimes of his nights. Seated in the high, backed chair bent over the little desk, he wrote... Today, on the little desk beside a large book is the famous coffee-pot of white porcelain and a cast of Balzac's hand.

Exactly ten years after the first encounter at Neuchâtel, Balzac debarked at St. Petersburg, going immediately to the home of Mme Hanska in the Kutaisoff house. After eight years of separation, the lovers now advanced towards one another beneath the elegant molding of the ceiling in the salon, where a large earthenware stove gave off some warmth. In this corpulent matron who had already brought seven children into the world, Balzac did not perceive the aging she had perhaps hoped to show him as justification for abandoning his dreams. He pronounced her more beatiful than ever.

There exist somewhat contradictory accounts of Balzac's physical aspect in adulthood. A friend of his, Caroline Marbouty, wrote to her mother from Italy: «His physique is ugly, his face beautifully expressive and strange.» Gavarni described him as «stupid, ignorant, dirty, ridiculous, opening his big eyes to everything that is said to him, at once naïve and astonishing in the knowledge he does not possess.» Work, more than age, bent his shoulders, swelled the pouches under his eyes, withered his skin and weightened his sedentary body.

Balzac, by David d'Angers: first design for a bust. «A masterpiece» (Balzac).

Mme Hanska, by Daffinger: the admirable work had been executed in Vienna, where the writer had gone to meet his friend. He had attended the posing sessions, and the painting pleased him enormously: «It speaks; one can speak with it. (It) will stay on my desk until the original is in my home.» And he confessed: «I reward myself (with this portrait) when I have done my work, and at night it is close to me and in it I seek my ideas.»

Dresden, where Balzac joined Mme Hanska in May 1945.
He described it as «a delightful city... part Swiss, part German.»
Six years earlier, Wagner had carried off his first success there.

◀ It seems quite possible that the novelist drew his self-portrait
in the depiction of his hero David Séchard, in *Illusions
perdues*: «...his head with its dark-skinned, ruddy, fleshy face,
supported by a thich neck enveloped in a dense forest of
black hair... (but)... in the furrows of his heavy lips, in the
dimple of his chin, in the shape of his square nose cleft by
a flat, tortured curve, and above all in his eyes, the constant
flame of a single passion and the sagacity of a thinker...»

In September 1847, Balzac went to Ukraine for the first time, to visit Mme Hanska on her property in Wierzchovnia: «Exactly like the Louvre,» exclaimed the writer. «An estate as large as a French département.»

The château of Mme Hanska.

◀ A dependence
of Mme Hanska's estate.

These paintings, published for the first time, represent various rooms of the apartments occupied by Mme Hanska, where Balzac kept her company. These aquarelles of minute precision were done by a Russian artist at the request of Mme Hanska when she left for Paris. She wished to preserve a souvenir of the place where she had lived.

On March 14, 1850, after long years of waiting – Mme Hanska had been a widow for nine years – the marriage was celebrated in the church of St. Barbara, at Berdichev, in Ukraine. Above, a view of the city at that time, in a painting preserved in the U.S.S.R (The first photograph of the painting.)

This striking portrait – the last – was executed at Tours by a friend of the writer, the Doctor Miquel whom they called «the poor man's doctor.» Balzac has evoked this worthy image of the doctor under his true name, in *Le Lys dans la Vallée.*

The mansion in the rue Fortunée, Paris, which Balzac had acquired in 1846 to use as his residence after his marriage with Mme Hanska. He wanted to furnish it lavishly: «If I do not become great with *La Comédie humaine, I shall be so with this achievement.*» He was not able to move in until four years later, only to die there the following year.
Situated near the Champs-Elysées, the building was demolished in 1882. Contrary to what Balzac thought, stones are more fragile than books!

In this letter, which attempts to be ironic but which reveals his naive pride, Balzac informs an old friend of his marriage: «On the fourteenth day of this month, one of the most eminent of prelates, delegated to represent the Bishop of Zytomir, blessed my union with Mme Eve, the Countess Rzewuska, now Mme Eva de Balzac. In becoming the husband of the great-niece of Marie Leczinska, the brother-in law of an aide-de-camp of His Majesty the Emperor of all the Russias, Count A. Rzewuski, brother-in-law of Count Orloff, the nephew of the Countess Rosalie Rzewuska..., etc., etc., I shall have to submit to a good deal of mockery; the newspapers will say I am cousin of the sun and son-in-law of the moon... but the fullest, most insolent happiness lies in feeding the public envy.»

The end of a great man. Balzac's death, in a moving engraving by Lix: «...A bed stood in the middle of the room... Monsieur de Balzac lay in this bed, his head resting on a mass of pillows to which had been added red damask cushions borrowed from the couch. His face was purple, almost black, and inclined to the right; he was unshaven, his hair gray and cropped, his eyes wide open and fixed. I saw him in profile and thus, he resembled the emperor.» (Victor Hugo, *Choses vues.*)

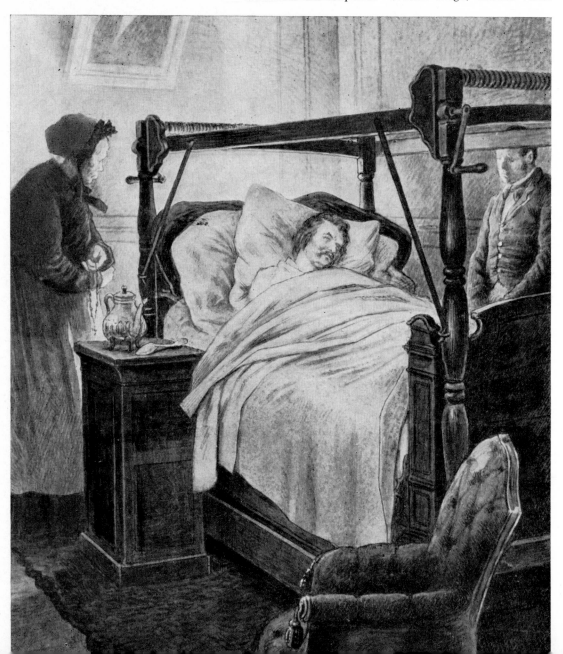

Balzac on his death-bed. At fifty-one he was a spent man. Already five years earlier, in 1846, weighed down by exhaustion and discouragement, he had written: «My brain has given out like a hobbled horse. I must resort to what I call masturbation of the mind. It is frightening.» The following year, aggravation: «I am left with neither heart nor soul; everything has died... I shall die exhausted, of work and anxiety... My weariness is incurable... I am getting thinner, I am interested in nothing... I lose myself more and more in the unending idleness of melancholy. I am unconscious of life; I no longer believe in the future.»

This room, photographed before the destruction of
the Balzac mansion, rue Fortunée in Paris – today
rue Balzac – was the novelist's bedroom, upon whose
walls he rested his final gaze.

Mme de Balzac, as widow. The little-known portrait
of the Countess in mourning dress was executed by
Gigoux.
After sixteen years of correspondence, Balzac enjoyed
only six months of conjugal life, and lived little
more than one year with the proud Eva, the Countess
Hanska, née Rzewuska.

The cast of Balzac's hand has often been reproduced; photographed here for the first time is the view of the palm, with its lines deeply significant for chirologists. Théophile Gautier has noted that Balzac's hands «were of a rare beauty, white, with small, chubby fingers and brilliant, rose-colored nails... The true hands of a prelate.» He adds that Balzac «was quite proud of them and smiled when someone would look at them.»

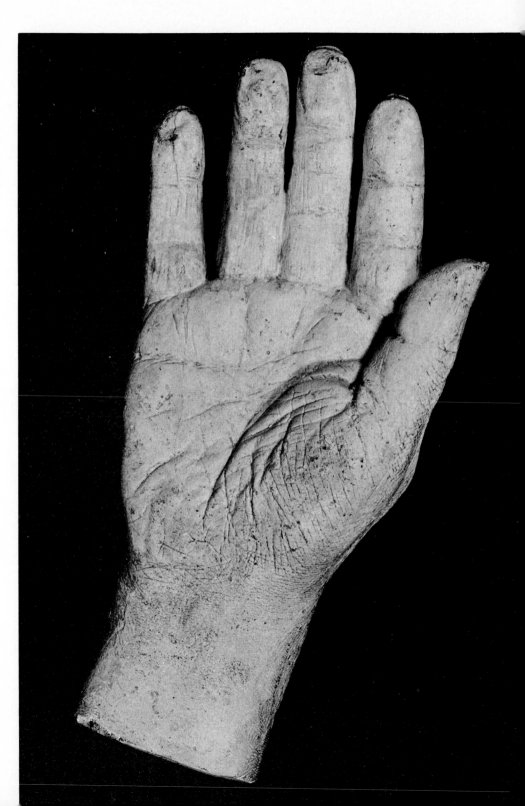

An essay for the statue of Balzac received as commission by Rodin from the Literary Society founded by the novelist. The monument was to be erected on a square in Paris, on the occasion of the writer's centenary. After having studied various portraits of the novelist, the sculptor took as model for the body and attitude a certain Tourangeau, a native of Azay-le-Rideau, having him pose on an estate in the environs of this charming town. Exhibited at the Salon of 1898, the work gave rise to passionate polemica and throughout several months, every day, it was the object of numerous articles in French and foreign newspapers: articles, for the most part, violently hostile. Surprised and pained, Rodin withdrew the statue from the Salon. Several art lovers offered him considerable sums of money, but he refused all propositions. Never did he imagine the glory this masterpiece would bring him later on.

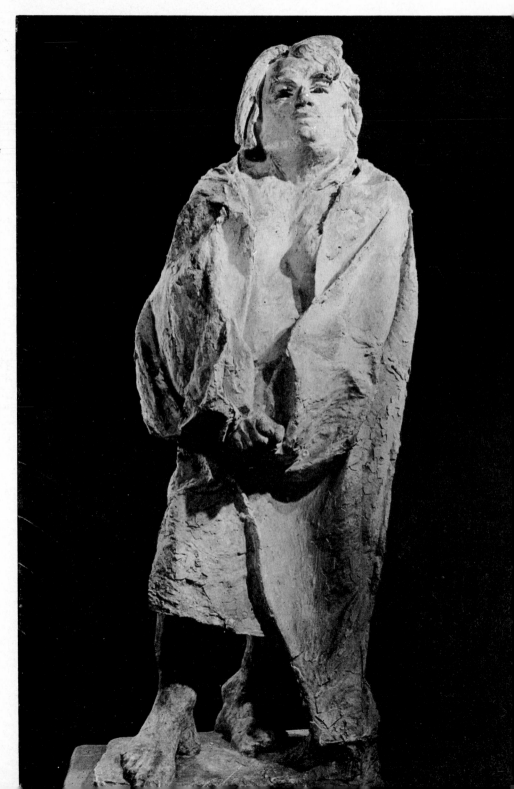

de Balzac (signature)

★ The critical pupil

In his study of the life and works of the novelist, André Bellesort relates:
«One of his comrades, godson of Mme de Stäel, translated (one day at school) the sentence *Caius Gracchus vir nobilis*, meaning "Caïus Gracchus, a man of the nobility" by: "Caïus Gracchus was of a noble heart."
» — Where do you see heart in *nobilis*? brusquely asked the professor. (And everyone laughed.) What would Mme the Baroness de Stäel say if she learned that you misinterpreted the word which signifies: of noble race, of patrician origin?
» — She would say that you are an idiot! said Honoré, half-aloud.
» — Sir poet, you will not be allowed to go out for eight days, said the professor, who had unfortunately heard him.»
In this anecdote, one finds a trait characteristic of Balzac: his passion for identifying the elite of humanity, «the noble hearts,» with the aristocracy.

★ «I shall be king»

When Balzac declared that he wanted to be a writer, his family had retorted:
— You seem to forget that in literature, those who do not attain royalty are nothing but miserable souls.
— Well then I shall be king, said he without hesitation.

★ Old man Dablin

Dablin, a friend of Honoré, was the ironmonger of his region. Although our young writer called him: «Good ol' man Dablin,» he was only thirty-seven years old, «but so serious and prudent that the irony of his friends described him well,» writes René Benjamin. «No one could be more dignified. The soul of honor. His complexion was gray, his forehead small, his disposition cold. However, as soon as he had the opportunity to render some service, or to speak of art and artists, he would suddenly radiate a naïve, pure warmth.» One can well understand Balzac's affection for him; he dedicated his first book to him.

★ Declaration to Mme de Berny

The declaration in a letter addressed to Mme de Berny by Honoré in 1832 merits mention:
«You are unhappy, I know; but you have in your soul undiscovered treasures that can still bring you closer to life. You will be surprised to learn that a young heart ordinarily filled with presumtuous feeling could have conceived, guarded, and nourished a passion without seeking to embellish it with the riches of hope. But thus I am, thus will I always be, timid to an extreme, in love to the point of delirium, and so chaste as to be incapable of uttering the words: I love. Within this chastity and modesty of sentiment enter all the fear and shame which cause my refusal. Never have I felt their presence so acutely, for never have I exposed myself. Today, for the first time, I hazard a depiction of what I feel.»

★ «My soul joined to yours...»

A short while later, the young man cried out his happiness:
«O Laure, I write to you on a night filled with you, enveloped in its silence and pursued by the memory of your delirious kisses, and what ideas can I have? You have taken them from me. Yes, my soul is joined to yours, and from now on you will walk by my side. Oh, I am surrounded by a tenderly enchanting and magic spell: I see nothing but the bench, I feel nothing but your gentle pressure, and the dried flowers in front

of me conserve their inebriating odor. You experience some fears and you express them in a tone that tears at my heart. Alas! I am sure of what I swore, for your kisses have changed nothing. Oh! yes, I am changed, I love you to distraction!»

★ Balzac as publisher

Contrary to what has been believed, the publisher Balzac did not take excessive risks; in fact, he published mainly the classics — the complete works of La Fontaine, for example, with thirty illustrations by Deveria. On the front cover: *H. Balzac, publisher-propietor*. In order to publish a complete Molière, he was obliged to take on a partner. These works did not obtain the success expected. Why? It was noticed that their text was abridged and perhaps this was not found so appealing.

★ Forty volumes in five years!

In one year alone, 1822, Balzac published five volumes: *L'Héritière de Birague, Jean-Louis, L'Israélite, Le Centenaire, Le Vicaire des Ardennes.* If he produced only one in 1823, *La Dernière Fée*, he then immediately continued on to two more, including *Argow le Pirate*, 1825, then the appearance of *Jeanne la Pâle, L'Excommunié*, and *Dom Gigadas*; these last two works are not absolutely ascribed to him, but it is most likely that he is their author. One must not think that he did not write much else during this period, for his sister attests to his having produced forty volumes only in five years.

★ «Rabelais was no good for him»

To her daughter Laure, Mme Balzac wrote this revealing lines:
«Our friends recognize that Honoré has a great deal of imagination, perhaps more so than he knows, but that he also lacks a certain judgment. He is often in the company of young people whose taste is not quite desirable and who forget the good they have been taught and never think that the idle talk they spread for laughter may have a great influence on someone like Honoré. Rabelais also is no good for him;

Sterne, too, does something that suspends common sense. In short, I am upset! Either he believes himself everything, or else *nothing at all*; his brain is in disorder, and I am afraid of writing him the things I tell you now... Mme de Berny, who is much taken by him, said to me the other day: «I am very much attached to him and I would give much to see that he is careful of his words, his attitudes, his tone!»

★ «What you mean to me»

The following letter reveals the kind of love Laure de Berny bore for Honoré: «I am so accustomed to living with you, not from day to day, but from minute to minute, that each one which enables me to enjoy your sweet presence becomes for me an entire existence; it absorbs everything, past and future, everything is contained in it... O my love... to remain in ecstasy, absorbed by memories is all that I can do; how can I tell you of my happiness? You would have to know yourself, and that is impossible, impossible to know all that you mean to me. Once, in a mad dream, I wished to be loved in a sublime way, but the fulfillment of this desire would have nothing in comparison with the riches you bring me.»

★ Quarrel with Latouche

After a long friendship, Balzac and the poet-novelist-(perhaps)-occultist Latouche had an argument. Honoré was unconstrained, Latouche was caustic. Following is the way in which the latter refused to house the writer at his small inn at Aulnay, near Robinson:
«Who would buy the provisions for an establishment of two people in the woods; who would fix the lunch and dinner for travelers? You? The day wouldn't be long enough to put things back in order. And a man like Honoré, of all people! who can't even wipe the table on which he writes! Good God, on the following day we'd tear out our hair.»
And then, since Honoré began multiplying his «author's revisions» for the first proof of *Le Dernier Chouan*:
«Your paper is so overloaded with words that the cost is augmented by one hundred crowns. Are you willing to pay them? You're a fine one! I'll gladly be your friend, but your publisher... never!»

92

A page of proof for Balzac's manuscript ... enough to make the best printer desperate. On December 15, 1837 *Le Figaro* published an amusing article on this subject: «... Imagine four or five hundred arabesques of this kind, intertwining, knotting, climbing and sliding from one margin to the other and from top to bottom. Picture twelve maps mixing up cities, rivers and mountains. Twine tangled by a cat, all the hieroglyphes of the Pharoahs' dynasties, all the fireworks of twenty celebrations! »At this sight, the printing shop finds little to be glad about. The type-setters strike their breast, the presses groan, the readers tear out their hair, the apprentices lose their heads. The more intelligent ones take a look at the proofs and recognize the Persian, others the writings of an ancient tribe, a few the symbolic language of Vishnu. They all work completely by chance and by the grace of God.»

George Sand said of Latouche that he «loved to teach, repeat, point out, but he wearied easily of the vain, and would turn his wit against them in derisive compliments whose malice no one could return.»

They named him Rivarol II; his dispute with Balzac took place in 1831.

★ A true friend

The following extracts of letters addressed to Balzac by Zulma Carraud reveal the latters's depth of friendship for him, and her spiritual qualities: «You are the best prose-writer of our time and for me, the best writer. You are unique and everything loses its color when compared to you... And yet, my dear, I hesitate to add my voice to the thousand voices which praise you...»

«I covet your perfection; it is altogether different from your «salon successes» or your vogue (I deplore these, for they will be your ruin for the future). No, what I am speaking of is your true glory, your future glory; I attach as much importance to it as I would if I bore your name or if I were close enough to you to feel its radiation about me.»

★ A country woman

In her correspondence, Zulma Carraud spoke also of herself: she was little satisfied with her children; her husband, a commander, was in poor health; Issoudun had not much to offer. More than one reader, perhaps, will recognize her own life in these lines written by that remarkable woman: «Often I have begun letters to you which I did not finish; I did not know how... My poor Honoré, I feel that I am inevitably becoming more materialistic, I am submitting to the influence of my surroundings. Vulgarity spreads around me like an oil spot, and I cannot remedy it. All that is coarse in manner and expression still revolts and irritates me to a great degree; but I can already see the time when I shall tolerate all of this patiently and philosophically.»

She was now only concerned with details, she said, something she abhorred; «and with what details, good God, all that occupies the town of Issoudun.»

★ A story, elegant and brutal...

As soon as it appeared, *La Peau de Chagrin* won considerable acclaim. No one could better speak of this major work than Jules Janin:

«Like a brigand, it surveys us, a pistol in one hand, a knife in the other: your money or your life? Analysis hurls itself and crashes head-on into a book like this; it is more than exotic, savory, elegant, colorful, and brutal. With this book, M. de Balzac has just placed himself among our leading story-tellers. I do not think that boldness of narration has ever attained so elevated a level. One is struck by blows, kisses, stings, voluptuousness, fire and iron. Such is *La Peau de Chagrin!*»

And Théophile Gautier very well perceived certain revolutionary aspects of the work: never before had an author dared to depict as in this book, a man in love who wonders, of course, whether he is loved as much, but who at the same time can be concerned about paying the coach-driver whose services he has engaged to return the beloved to her home. A detail indeed certain to shock the public of that time!

★ Sweetness of Touraine

The gentle slopes of the Loire, the city of Tours, the valley of the Cher: somewhere Balzac wrote that these constituted «all his childhood treasures.» «Do not ask me why I love Touraine,» he said, «I love it as an artist loves art.» Equally happy was he during his stay at «La Grenadière»; there he was in the company of his beloved Mme de Berny. The property was located at Saint-Cyr-sur-Loire; from there one could perceive the neighboring town and the well-loved river.

Here the lovers passed a part of the summer 1830, then went down the Loire by boat to Croisic: at this time the Loire was still navigable!

Subsequently, Balzac wished to buy «La Grenadière,» which he compared to a valuable jewel. But this and other dreams of ownership disappeared in the consuming fire of Parisian life and of his inhuman career as a novelist.

He chose the name of «La Grenadière» for the title of one of his short stories.

★ Napoleon: a good affair

One day, Balzac sold a manuscript to an acquaintance of his, a former hosier named Gaudy who desired to obtain the Legion of Honor. The man could publish the book under his name and dedicate it to Louis-Philippe, which would certainly get him the coveted award. This curious transaction brought him four thousand francs.

What book did it concern? It was a collection of Napoleon's thoughts. Balzac had jotted them down on a large pad over a period of seven years: «Every time I read a book about Nopaleon in which I found an interesting quote of his, I would write it down in (this) notebook.»

«On a day of distress, with no money in my pocket, I counted how many there were. There were five hundred, making it the most beautiful book of the age.»

★ The effects of coffee

Balzac's description of the effects of coffee, which he consumed in immense quantities:

«(After you drink some) everything becomes agitated; ideas are set in motion like army battalions on the battlefields, and then the battle begins. Memories charge forward, banners flying; the light cavalry of comparisons progresses at a magnificent gallop; the artillery of logic hastens into the fray with its cannons and cartridges...»

★ Egoism of the thinking man

To the kindly Zulma Carraud he said:

«...My life is a struggle; step by step I must fight for the recognition of my talent, if there be any. And then, the pain of privations is not justified. No pleasures whatsoever! To think that there are women today who write to me from all over, complimenting me and thinking me surrounded by delights, but most frequently, just curious and crafty! Ah! don't play the judge; I have often thought of you and if I have not written more often, the fault is that of my cruel life. The egoism of a man who lives by thinking is something awful. To be a man apart from others, one must begin by truly placing himself apart...»

96

Balzac and his horse, an amusing sketch by Delacroix. The worldly attitudes of the writer annoyed the great painter who nonetheless admired his talent. For his part, Balzac sent Delacroix his books and admiration. Besides a horse, Balzac owned a tilbury of which he was very proud. Unfortunately it was seized as payment in a lost lawsuit.

★ One hundred oysters, twelve cutlets... and the rest

André Billy, in his important work on Balzac has written:

«Temperate when alone, he displayed a lavishness and the appetite of an ogre in society. Werdet (one of his publishers) attests to having seen him at one sitting swallow one hundred oysters, twelve cutlets au jus, a duckling with turnips, a pair of roasted partridges, accompanied by various side-dishes, followed by a dozen pears soaked in the most delicate of wines, not forgetting, of course, the coffee and liqueurs.

»One drank stiffly under his roof, but this pleasure readily assumed with him a romantic and literary form. Each bottle taken from the cellar had its own history. One had made the tour of the world, another dated from a fabulous epoch, this rum issued from a barrel which had rolled around on the high seas for a hundred years and then had to be attacked with an ax, so thick was the layer of shells and sea-weed that surrounded it... The wine perhaps had gone sour, the incredulous guests had restrained a smile, but Balzac did not crack a smile.»

His friend and contemporary, Théophile Gautier, remarked with reason that the novelist gave «signs of violent health, in little keeping with the romantic palor in vogue.» In effect:

«His lips palpitated, his eyes alighted with pleasure, and his hands trembled with joy at the sight of a pyramid of pears and fat peaches... He was a superb pantagruelesque sight, with his loosened tie, his open shirt, fruit knife in hand, smiling and drinking...»

André Billy continues, «(he) attached more importance to the container than to the contents, to the silverware and the dishes than to the food. A list made by his silversmith, Lecointe, mentions five silver platters, twelve teaspoons, «a fish-carver, with silver handle,» four salt-cellars and a mustard pot with «silver-gilt interior,» a large serving spoon, and a «silver teapot, English style.» All in all it was worth no more than four thousand francs, which did not prevent him from soon going to the pawnshop. For a less striking, totally different aspect of prodigality: during a stay in Saché (Touraine), he suddenly needed a pair of leather gloves. He forthwith wrote to his publisher Gosselin, asking him to send twelve pair, which he would reimburse with a short story.»

In this absurd and capricious fancy for food and useless objects, in this anxiety to appear wealthy and noble, or to feel himself thus, a psychoanalist would probably see the result of frustration due to the absence of maternal love during childhood.

As an example of another famous worker and eater, whose behavior was however less neurotic, one can cite Victor Hugo whose appetite was the admiration of his contemporaries and whose titanic work was doubled by a considerable epistolary, journalistic, and political activity.

★ Love in silk

The robust Tourangeau conceived of love only in refinement; as is proved by the following excepts from *La Peau de Chagrin*:

«I admit, shamefacedly, that I cannot conceive of love in misery. Perhaps there is in me a depravity due to that human disease which we call civilization; nevertheless a woman, be she as attractive as the beautiful Helen of Homer, loses all power over my senses as soon as she shows even the slightest bit of gutter dirt. Ah! Long live love in silk and on cashmir rugs, surrounded by the wonders of luxury that array it in splendor, for it is perhaps a luxury in itself. I love to feel the wrinkle of fine clothes crushed beneath my desires, to bruise flowers, to lay my devastating hands upon the elegant edifice of perfumed heads. Irresistibly, I am drawn to bright eyes, hidden behind a veil of lace pierced by a look as the smoke of cannons is torn by the flame. My love seeks a silken ladder climbed in silence on a winter's night. What a pleasure to arrive covered with snow and to enter a room laden with scents and hung with painted tapestries.»

«In France, fortunately for me, we have been without a queen for twenty years; I would have loved the queen.»

★ Recourse to hypnotism

We already know what kind of sojourn Balzac had with Mme de Castries at Aix-les-Bains. She was quite willing to play the game and even enrolled at the hotel as Mme de Balzac; but although Honoré dowsed himself with strong perfume and changed gloves every day, he did not get any farther. This refusal only served to exasperate all the more this unhappy fellow. Bewildered, on his return to Paris he went to consult a hypnotist named Chapelain. It is amusing to remark that as a preliminary step, Balzac gave to the man a piece of cloth worn by the Duchess and bearing a trace of her perfume. Unfortunately, it all came to nothing.

★ «When you will miss your duchesses...»

In response to Balzac's bitter letter about his disappointment at Aix, Zulma Carraud, who had counselled him in the affair sent him these lines:

«Why did I send you to Aix, Honoré? Because there alone could you find what you needed... You desire a woman of fleeting forms, with intoxicating manners, a true kind of elegance, and in this satin envelope, you hope to find a generous and colorful spirit. That cannot be... I let you go to Aix because we have not one thought in common, because I scorn what you deify, because I shall never be able to conceive how someone whose glory is all made can sacrifice it *to money*. You are in Aix because you must be bought by an offer and a woman is the price of this market; because your soul is warped, because you have repudiated the true glory for *vain glory*. When you will miss your duchesses, I shall still be there, offering you the consolation of sincere sympathy.»

★ Mme de Castries' defense

Balzac wrote to Mme de Castries herself with a violent tone, reproaching her for the abuse of his honesty and love, using them to serve political ends, raising his hopes and then withdrawing at the last moment. She defended herself:

«What a horrible letter you wrote to me! One never sees the woman who received it! One never sees the man who conceived it! You have hurt me; must I therefore excuse myself? I am wrong to write in such agitation. How you break a heart already broken! A heart which gave you all its affection; a heart exhausted from sorrow which asked you, ah! no, I cannot express what transpires within me. Why do you bring tears to those eyes which have already cried so much? Farewell, if I have hurt you, you avenge yourself cruelly.» On the essence of the grief, not a word...

843.701
D34h

3 84110000 5164

76. 3-351

With his bulky baboon silhouette, his blue suit with gold buttons, his famous cane like a golden crowbar and his abundant, disheveled hair, Balzac was a sight for caricature. The specialists went to it wholeheartedly, the malevolent critics mocked at his pretentions, his awkwardness, his belly and false coat of arms; it was the vermin in the beast's den ... Everywhere he went he brought his penetrating, pensive glance, his marvelous eyes, like those of a lion, streaked with gold, brown and devouring.

101

HIGHLAND COMMUNITY
JUNIOR COLLEGE LIBRARY
HIGHLAND, KANSAS

★ The first letter to Mme Hanska

«If only you knew with what force a solitary spirit rejected by everyone
rushes toward a true affection! I love you, my stranger, and this bizarre
thing is nothing but the natural result of a life forever empty and
unhappy... Already I love you too much without having seen you.
Certain passages of your letter made my heart beat; oh, if only you
knew with what ardor I fly towards that which I so long have desired,
of what devotion I am capable! The most delicate and romantic of
dreams nourished by a woman find in my heart, not an echo, but an
unbelievable simultaneity of thought. Forgive my price in misery and
my naiveté of suffering.»
«A life forever empty and unhappy»:— Who knew better than he?
It was a cry.

★ Balzac and Jean-Jacques

Those two great names of French literature, Balzac and Rousseau, those two
extraordinary, fascinating men – who would think of relating them? The
differences between them seem fundamental. It is only more interesting
to know that Balzac was well acquainted with Rousseau. Better still:
in one of his letters to Mme de Berny, he did not hesitate to compare
himself to his predecessor! («Never shall I better draw my character than it
has been by a great man. Read again *Les Confessions* and you will find
it therein.») Moreover, he had personal opinions on the adventures of
the Citizen of Geneva; for example, in his opinion, Jean-Jacques
«betrayed» Mme de Warens. On visiting Neuchâtel (where he first saw
Mme Hanska), he was drawn irresistibly to the island of Saint-Pierre, high
point in Rousseau's life. The impression left by this excursion was so
profound that «there are days when the memory of Saint-Pierre makes
me tremble.»

★ A ruse

Stefan Zweig, a biographer of Balzac, relates: «After the love letter
intercepted by Monsieur Hanska, Balzac was obliged to invent an excuse:
he had ceded to the Countess' wish to possess a love letter in elegant
French. He wrote to the Count to plead this lie.

»Even if Mme Hanska woud grant him "a generous and unreserved pardon," he would never forgive himself for having bruised and wounded for an instant this noble soul: 'I am probably destined never to see you again and I am profoundly regretful. So great an affection is not lost without many tears.'

»Far from excusing himself before the Count, Balzac with admirabile skill, invited the deceived husband to ask him to continue the correspondence with his wife and to persist in the preservation of a serene friendship.'»
(*Balzac*, by S. Zweig.)

★ Literature and Speculation

In the course of a dinner, whose guests were eager to hear the thoughts he was capable of emitting, Balzac spoke at great length about the structures he employed to exploit his work. After a while, his hostess, an aristocratic foreigner, could not refrain from saying:

— It seems to me that in your country, literature is an object of speculation. And Balzac answered:

— It is nothing but an object of speculation!

★ Balzac's accounts

Not only was Balzac extraordinary in his prodigality, but also in his economy! More astonishing yet was his imagination in either of the domains. Now he would pride himself on living on forty cents a day; at other times he would claim that in order to live as he wished, he needed three hundred thousand francs a month. One day, exasperated by his lack of realism, Théophile Gautier burst out: «Balzac, let's take a pencil and a sheet of paper, and let's draw up a budget. What would you do with 300,000 francs a month?» Balzac set down the most sumptuous wardrobe, the most opulently furnished mansions, the most expensive dancers at the Opera, a table of lucullus; in a generous spirit, Gautier granted him everything. Despite all Balzac's efforts, the fabulous total could not be reached. Théo already smiled triumphantly; 25,000 francs remained.

Therefore our great man said «Oh well! That will be for butter and radishes! What house *with a bit of decency* does not consume 25,000 francs of butter and radishes every month?» Théophile Gautier was speechless.

★ At the «Bon Hotel»

Furious at having to waste his time in the National Guard, an obligation of the citizens in his time, Balzac became a deserter. This finally cost him his imprisonment at the jail on the quai d'Austerlitz, called the *Bon Hotel*. He begged Werdet, then his publisher, to come to visit him. As he was dining with the latter in the refectory, the elegant Eugène Sue appeared.

«— My dear Eugène, exclaimed Honoré, come share the dinner with my publisher and me. We shall drink to our unexpected encounter.

«— Thank you, Honoré. My valet accompanied by my servants will bring me my meal.

Red with humiliation, Balzac sat down again, while two huge fellows hastened to serve his rival.

At that moment, the door of the refectory opened, giving way to the Count Lestange, editor-in-chief of the *Quotidienne,* who ran to Balzac, hands outstretched and seated himself at the table... The dinner was extremely cheerful; Balzac had had his revenge.

André Billy, who narrates this incident, also tells how, on the following day, Balzac's cell was filled with flowers and provisions, and how the obliging Werdet opened for him the enormous pile of letters from admirers. The next day, a party of eight gathered to celebrate, including Alphonse Karr, Sandeau, Gustave Planche, served by Balzac's liveried valet. With the dessert, Balzac was handed the gift of an admirer: the long blond (scented) hair of a woman, looped through a golden ring set with an emerald. It was not the only jewel; Balzac received enough to have one of his canes inlaid!

★ Balzac and occultism

Balzac, who consulted a hypnotist, preserved all his life a passion for the occult (to which he had been introduced by the Chevalier de Beauvoir). He was an avid believer in the most irrational and insane illuminism,

GARDE NATIONALE
DE PARIS.

MAISON D'ARRÊT.
Nº 168.44

CERTIFICAT D'ÉCROU.

SORTIE

Je certifie que le Sieur *De Balzac, Honoré Littérateur*
demeurant rue *Cassini* nº
1ᵉ Légion, *3ᵉ* Bataillon, *1ʳᵉ* Compagnie de *Chasseurs*
condamné à subir *48 heures* de prison, par décision
du Conseil ⁓ ⁓ ⁓ de discipline de ladite Légion, en date
du *2 Janvier 1835* est entré à la maison d'arrêt et
de discipline de la Garde nationale de Paris,
le *2 avril 1836* heure de *10h30* du Matin, et
qu'il y est resté *jusqu'à Ce jour même heure*

Paris, ce *29 avril 1836*

LE CONCIERGE DE LA MAISON D'ARRÊT,

Balzac refused to waste his time in the National Guard, so he was condemned by its
disciplinary counsel to three prison sessions, amounting to about a week's sentence.
He fulfilled the three at one time, in 1836.

running after faith-healers, soothsayers and other charlatans. One day, when Alfred de Musset had presented him to the directors of the very Catholic and very royalist *Gazette de France,* he proceeded to state:

‹– The eighteenth century was quite wrong in doubting the miracles of Jesus Christ. I am ready to defend Christianity against everyone and everything for...

The smile of these gentlemen froze when he finished with:

‹– ...I who am speaking to you have cured by the imposition of my hands!

With less of a gross naiveté, for here he put his finger on the still poorly known mechanism of intuition, he wrote: ‹That certain beings have the ability to perceive future events in the germ of their causes, as the great inventor perceives an industry or a science springing from a natural effect unseen by the ordinary man – it is not one of these powerful exceptions that clamor for attention; it is the effect of a recognized faculty which, in some sort, becomes the somnambulism of the mind.› Who knows if Balzac's destiny hadn't been announced to him, if he did not already know it?

★ Names real and fictitious

His taste for the occult led Balzac to behave like an alchemist of the Middle Ages who sought to endow life with *hormoncules* or mandrate roots. For him, the creation of romantic characters gave rise to magic, and often, during the course of his nocturnal hallucinations, it seemed to him that Eugénie Grandet or the Père Goriot were about to knock on the door and enter the room. He was also interested in proper names, on which subject he had precise ideas, as shown by Laure de Surville:

‹My brother had a singular theory on names; he claimed that fictitious names instilled no life into imaginary beings, whereas those which really existed bestowed reality. Thus he would gather names for *La Comédie humaine* wherever he went... Matifat! Cordot! What delightful names! he would exclaim to me. I found Matifat rue de la Perle. I can already see my Matifat! He will have the pale countenance of a cat, a petty bourgeois, for Matifat will have no grandeur, believe me. And Cordot! That's another matter! A good-natured chap as dry as a pebble, all lively and merry.›

Balzac himself once wrote: ‹Look at this name: L. Marcas! The man's entire life is contained in the fantastic assemblage of these seven letters. Seven! The most significant of cabalistic numbers. The man died at the age of thirty-five, thus his life was composed of seven stories. Marcas! Do you not get the idea of something precious which shatters in a fall, with or without noise?» He continued: «We are named from above before being so here below.» He had discovered this theory in the writings of Sterne, author of *Tristam Shandy* (whom Mme Balzac had accused, along with Rabelais, of «disordering Honoré's mind»).

★ Balzac the psychiatrist

«It is above all in neuro-pathology that he (Balzac) established himself as an innovator, and I do not fear to use term «prophet». Some of his descriptions, in their accuracy and minuteness of detail, fill us with admiration. In first rank is the psychosis of Louis Lambert. Doctor Devic, a psychiatrist from Lyon, writes that eighty years before Bleuler, Balzac had discerned the symptoms of a new disease, precocious insanity.» (Dr. Holte, quoted by G. Sigaux: *Balzac, Father of his Century*.)
This observation can be related to the criticism made of Dostoiewsky's *The Idiot* by a psychiatrist of our acquaintance; this doctor states that the character of the Idiot was impossible in an epileptic, his personality stemming rather from a feeble brain, for example. Who would have thought it? Of the two, Dostoiewsky eulogized by the fervents of psycho-pathological literature, and Balzac, the jolly fellow, the epicurean, the «realist,» it would be Balzac who shed a more revealing light on the case of psychosis!

★ The natural-born son of Balzac

The beautiful Sarah Guiroboni Visconti gave birth to Balzac's son on May 29, 1836. Lambinet claims that her husband, the Count-apothecary and music lover, had as his only reaction the following words:
—Ah! I knew that Madame wanted a dark-complexioned child. Well, she has one.
Boyer de la Martinière took it much more seriously. Protesting against the attribution of parenthood to this wretch Honoré, he received this answer from Mme Doumerc, a banker's wife:
—Sir, *I saw him do it.*

★ Théophile Gautier, the «journalist...»

With respect to the good Théophile Gautier and more precisely, to his literary activity, Balzac declared: «He is one of the talented men I recognize, but he lacks the power of conception... He has a lovely style, a great deal of wit, and I believe he will never accomplish anything.»
Why? «Because he is in journalism.»

★ Very Simple!

When the Theatre of l'Odéon accepted *Les Ressources de Quinola*, Balzac's best play, the director Lireu asked to what address he should send rehearsal announcements. Gozlan, who was present at the time, tells that Balzac became agitated; his address must remain unknown, as a result of his problems with creditors whom he avoided by all kinds of tricks, including a secret exit, like Vidocq in his tunnel. The following arrangement was finally reached: Every morning the theatre messenger would go with the bulletin to the Champs-Elysées. From the fountain of the Rond-point, he would head in the direction of the Arc de Triomphe, counting twenty trees on the left. At the twentieth he would see a man searching for a blackbird among the branches. Approaching he would say, «I have it» and the man answered: «If you have it, what are you waiting for?» The messenger then handed over the bulletin and the stranger would take off without turning his head. If by chance lightning struck the twentieth tree, the boy would go to the twenty-first.

★ Balzac and George Sand

During a stay at Frapesle, in February 1838, Balzac went to visit George Sand at Nohant. He found her by the fire, in dressing-gown, red pants, and yellow Turkish slippers, puffing on a cigar. He knew her well and noticed that her beautiful tawny skin was still fresh and her eyes black and sparkling. «We talked like old friends,» said Balzac. He had judged her unfavorably at the time of her separation from Sandeau, and he now reproached himself. How he detested Liszt, and how delighted he was at the idea of writing a novel about the Franz-George-Marie d'Agoult trio. During their long conversation, George Sand had said proudly: «Since we

A report written in Milan, March 2, 1837: Balzac's watch had been stolen ...

«At 4:30, on arriving by the contrada Magnani at the Piazza San Fedele, corner of the Inn Bella Venezia, a rather tall young man fell upon me and seized my watch by the chain.

»Four rubies. Form of the chain: (design).

»The chain is worth 500 francs, the watch 800. The numbers on the dial are Roman numerals. The key is of gold, and suspended by two little chains of the same model as the large one.

Honoré de Balzac.»

are preparing a revolution for the mores of the future, I am less struck by the inconveniences of marriage than by those of liberty.» Balzac, who detested stimulants other than those in cofee, returned from this visit madly smoking *houka*.

In honor of this latest mania, Lucien de Rubempré and Esther Gobseck smoked it too.

★ The last dialogue

Several times during his last days, Balzac had sent for the curé of Saint-Philippe-du-Roule, since Dr. Nacquart said of him that in his mouth religion was no more than the highest expression of the intelligence of the universe. Two hours before the beginning of his agony, Honoré received extreme unction from him. He did not altogether lose consciousness for on the final day, at dawn, he spoke with Nacquart and their brief conversation is recorded by Mirabeau:

«Balzac was choking. Yet between his gasps for breath, he asked Nacquart: «Tell me the truth, how do I stand?» Nacquart hesitated. At last he answered: «You are lost.» A light quiver ran through Balzac's face and his fingers clawed at the sheet. His only response: «Ah!» and then, a little later: «When must I die?» With his eyes full of tears, the doctor answered: «You may not last the night», and then they were silent.»

BULLOZ: 37 a and b — 39 — 40 — 44 — 46 a — 48 a —
49 — 50 a — 51 b — 52 a — 56 b — 57 — 58 b —
60 a — 61 a — 63 a — 68 — 69 — 70 b. BIBLIOTHÈQUE
NATIONALE PARIS: 56 a — 67 a — 70 a. — S. KNECHT:
53 — 54 b. COLLECTION LOVENJOUL: 55 — 59 b. MAISON
DE BALZAC: 33 a — 34 a and b — 43 a and b — 45 a
and b — 47 b — 58 a — 62 a — 65 a and b — 66 —
71 b — 74 — 78 a — 79. MUSÉE HISTOIRE DE L'EDUCA-
TION, PARIS: 36 a and b — 38. MUSÉE RODIN, PARIS:
80 © by Spadem 1965. MUSÉE DE SACHÉ: 33 b — 47 a —
48 b — 52 b — 59 a — 62 b — 71 a — 72 a and b —
73 b — 75 — 76 — 77. ROGER-VIOLLET: 35 — 41 a and
b — 42 a and b — 60 b — 61 b — 67 b. TOURISME
SUISSE: 50 b — 51 a. A. WURMSERS 73 a.

Printed in Spain

Printed by Editorial Bruguera, S. A.
Mora la Nueva, 2 - Barcelona (6) - Spain

Depósito Legal B 40.134 - 1969